Paul Harris

Improve your teaching!

an essential handbook for instrumental and singing teachers

includes Paul Harris's innovative strategy –
'Simultaneous Learning'

FABER *ff* MUSIC

Cover images courtesy of The National Foundation for Youth Music –
a UK-wide charity set up to provide high quality and diverse music-making
opportunities for 0 to 18-year-olds who would not otherwise get the chance.
Also thanks to Emily Behague.

© 2006 by Faber Music Ltd
First published in 2006 by Faber Music Ltd
3 Queen Square London WC1N 3AU
Design by Susan Clarke
Printed in England by Caligraving Ltd

ISBN 0-571-52534-2

To buy Faber Music publications or to find out about the full range of titles available
please contact your local music retailer or Faber Music sales enquiries:
Faber Music Limited, Burnt Mill, Elizabeth Way, Harlow, CM20 2HX, England
Tel: +44 (0) 1279 82 89 82   Fax: +44 (0) 1279 82 89 83
sales@fabermusic.com   fabermusic.com

Contents

Foreword

Paul Harris believes that teaching music should always be a joy. This book brilliantly communicates the remarkable energy and enthusiasm that has made him one of the great reflective practitioners of our time. Within these pages his fascination with the teaching process proves to be truly inspirational. Paul proposes a style of teaching – 'Simultaneous Learning' – that allows both tutor and pupil to embark on what he describes as 'an invigorating, untroubled, absorbing and stimulating journey'. Teachers are invited to find the courage to ask self-searching questions, to look for new ideas, to adapt and change and to take a real pride in their work. In turn, pupils will gain a new understanding of every aspect of what they are doing. The music lesson becomes a voyage of discovery, where a pupil's spirits are raised and confidence increases; thus the teaching and learning experience will always be positive and effective.

Paul encourages problem solving from as many different angles as possible, taking into account the preferences of different types of learning styles. The breadth of this holistic approach has the potential for rich rewards, as pupils begin to think musically for themselves. Operating an instrument counts for little without musical expression, creativity or imagination. During the course of his exceptionally sympathetic text, Paul emphasises the importance of creating confidence – an empowering self-belief that develops slowly but surely and results in poise, humility and self-assurance.

It was during the generation before Mozart that the great German flautist J. J. Quantz wrote that many musicians of his acquaintance had agile fingers but were reluctant to use their brains. Such sentiments have resonated ever since within the senior common rooms of schools, conservatoires and universities. This book contains an exciting and convincing agenda for redressing the balance. It will surely revolutionise the teaching of music at all levels.

Colin Lawson MA (Oxon), MA, PhD, DMus, FRCM, FLCM
Director, Royal College of Music

Introduction

I've always loved teaching. In the professional world there can be few joys greater than unlocking potential and helping aspiring musicians develop their abilities. And I've always been fascinated by the process of teaching, which is where this book comes in. It's a book about teaching. In particular it is about 'Simultaneous Learning' – a style of teaching that engages both pupil and teacher fully, removing all obstacles along the way to allow both parties to enjoy an invigorating, untroubled, absorbing and stimulating journey.

The 'Simultaneous' approach permeates all areas of teaching, whatever aspect of music you are working on – from your first lesson with a new pupil to your most advanced students. Once you've digested the main principles outlined in chapter two, you'll discover it becomes the major driving force behind all areas of music teaching.

I hope you'll find the approach energising and helpful, and that it will begin to unlock doors as well as open up all sorts of new and exciting avenues to pursue in your own teaching.

A few personal words ...

In my work all over the world I continually meet teachers, some of whom I would call – without hesitation – inspirational. I have learnt so much from talking to them, observing their work and listening to their pupils.

I have also been exceptionally lucky to count among my own teachers some truly inspirational musicians. Alan Taylor who taught me at school, Graeme Humphrey at the Royal Academy of Music and Professor Keith Swanwick at the University of London. There are certain friends who continually provide me with a clear ambition: Richard Crozier, whose humour and clarity of thought have been a constant driving force; Tony Meredith, who read the manuscript and made many invaluable suggestions; Sally Adams, Mike Brewer, Jean Cockburn, Esther Jackson, Brian Ley, Irene Lock, Melanie Ragge and Robert Tucker, who have all offered much support and many words of wisdom and advice. Richard King, Beth Millett, Kathryn Oswald and Leigh Rumsey at Faber Music, whose continuous encouragement has been awesome. And especially Professor John Davies who has been a continual friend and mentor from my very first lesson. Also other friends and pupils – they know who they are – without whose help this book would not exist. To all, huge thanks.

UK/USA terminology
aural = ear training
bar = measure
crotchet = quarter note
term = semester

1 We can all improve our teaching ...

... if we really want to. Being a great teacher doesn't happen by accident. Teachers become great through care, planning, hard work, skill, imagination and through the continuing desire for personal improvement. To be a great teacher you need to be hungry – hungry for knowledge, for feeding your imagination, for developing your personality. You need to be prepared to invest time (and perhaps even money!) in personal development. It will repay you enormously. Great teachers are great learners and learning is a lifelong activity.

If you do what you've always done, you'll get what you've always got

If you're satisfied with that; if you feel that your pupils are doing as well as they possibly can; if you feel there's no room for any more self-improvement – then this book is not for you. If, on the other hand, you are excited by the thought of 'maximising your potential', then read on!

Being a great instrumental[1] teacher is a state of mind. It develops from a confidence that itself develops from understanding – an intuitive, instinctive understanding of how the various elements of music fit together; of how to access and use your imagination; how to see beneath the surface; how to hear what others might not; and of how to bring teaching and learning vividly to life.

Are you prepared to change?

Self-improvement may (and probably will) require change. Most of us are slightly apprehensive about change; indeed some of us go to great lengths to avoid even the slightest change to our routine. Human beings are creatures of habit – in general we do the same things each day, eat the same foods, take the same routes, park in the same spot in the supermarket (and feel annoyed if someone else has parked in our spot!), teach each pupil in roughly the same way. To develop you will need to commit to change – or, to begin with, at least the idea of change. (Otherwise even if you do read this book, setting out with good intentions, nothing much will happen.) Have the courage to try out new ideas. Dare to do things differently and to be different. Gently and little by little is fine – don't feel you need to change too much. Dip your toes into new water; make the process a gradual one. Try out new ideas alongside your own tried and tested ones but don't just continue to do what you've always done.

The here and now

As a lesson progresses we constantly have to make decisions about what to say and what to do next. Many of our reactions and decisions will be automatic, as will much of our use of language and vocabulary. We will fall back on tried and tested strategies; we often live in what some call our 'comfort zone' but

[1] I once spoke to a singing teacher who was adamant that singers use the voice as an instrument. So all references to 'instrumental' include singing too.

living there may be restricting and a strategy that may work for some pupils may not work for others.

At your next lesson, step outside yourself and try to observe your teaching objectively – see the bigger picture. Listen to the language and words you use. Be aware of how you react and how your pupils respond, be aware of how the lesson is developing and of how much *musical* activity there is. Make a note of what you feel was successful and anything you feel could have gone better. Do this at least once or twice a day for a while. How satisfied are you with your conclusions?

While we're about it, here are some other important questions. Spend some quality time thinking about them and about the significance of your answers. Return to these questions often. They ought constantly to be in your mind.

- How passionate are you about your teaching? Put yourself on a scale of one to ten – and be honest! (Ten equals very passionate.)
- How do you think your pupils see you? (Friendly, supportive, caring, serious, humorous, enthusiastic, grumpy, scary, confident, knowledgeable?) How would you like them to see you?
- When teaching, do you always enjoy your work or do you occasionally find yourself getting bored, sometimes even frustrated with certain pupils?
- Why are you teaching?

Teaching music should always be a joy. If it is, then the ideas in this book should help you inspire your pupils even more. If it's not, then it's time for serious thinking and perhaps some serious change. If you're really committed to improving your teaching, then you'll have to be willing to change some of your habits and teaching strategies which you may have been using and relying on for years. Don't feel unsettled by the thought of change but rather be challenged, excited and exhilarated.

I have been evolving and refining the teaching method outlined in this book over a number of years (and that refining process still continues). I haven't discovered an entirely new way to teach but rather given a name to an approach familiar to many good teachers and shown how to develop the various ideas in what I hope is an imaginative and stimulating way.

Let's begin by having a closer look at our teaching as it is now and then begin to explore new and exciting ways forward.

Know your instrument

If you want to teach really well, you must know and love your instrument. You don't have to be the world's greatest player but you do need to keep up your enthusiasm. Learn new pieces (perhaps those that you are teaching). Try to play in ensembles and orchestras, accompany friends, sing in choirs. Go to concerts, buy new CDs and listen to old favourites played by different performers. Listen to new music on the radio. Explore technique – search for new fingerings, new solutions to old problems. Perhaps even have a lesson from someone you admire from time to time. Broaden your knowledge of the repertoire, get to know your instrument's history and how it works. Yes this all takes time but with good organisation you will undoubtedly be able to set aside some time each week to develop and deepen your own understanding and insight. It's *very* important.

A time for reflection and setting new standards

At the end of every lesson we should try to set aside a moment or two for reflection – 'so … was that a good lesson?' 'Was it *good enough*?' 'Could it have been better?' We should *always* have that desire to give an even better lesson next time. And that doesn't necessarily mean that we haven't given a good lesson this time! There is always room for improvement.

In general, many teachers are probably delivering lessons that range between just about acceptable to reasonably good. Either way, is that really satisfactory? Trying to improve your teaching means thinking a lot, reflecting on what goes well, what doesn't and why. It means getting your hands on the latest books on your subject, searching the internet for interesting articles, attending relevant conferences, talking about teaching with other teachers, observing good teaching practice, watching your peers at work, caring more and always desiring to deliver the best lesson you can. What will this lead to? Your pupils will respect and work harder for you, parents will seek you out to teach their children and your self-esteem will rise, as indeed will your quality of life.

In this way you are becoming what is known as a *reflective practitioner* – having the courage to ask self-searching questions, always on the look out for new ideas, happy to adapt or change and taking a real pride in what you do. The first important step forward has been made.

2 Simultaneous Learning

The first principle

Find a blank sheet of paper and make a list of all the various aspects that *ought* to be included in your lessons. Here's one to get you going: 'teaching pieces or songs'. Playing or singing pieces is what the majority of our pupils enjoying doing most and on the whole they are what we most enjoy teaching!

Don't read on until you've made your list – it will only take you a couple of minutes!

Here is my list based on discussions with teachers at seminars around the world. How many of the following are in your list? Can you think of any more?

- Teacher talking and pupil/s talking
- Teaching pieces/songs; ensemble work
- Aural work, listening, clapping, singing, internalising
- Theory
- Posture, warm-ups (and downs!) and technical work
- Scales and arpeggios
- Rhythm
- Notation work
- Sight-reading
- Improvisation
- Composition
- Teaching pupils how to practise effectively
- Teaching pupils to evaluate their work
- Having fun!

That's all very well (you'll be thinking) but how can I manage more than a few of those in a ten/twenty/thirty minute lesson? There is a way but first here's another question for you:

What did you have to eat the evening of the night before last?

Don't read on until you've remembered!

To have arrived at your answer you probably steered yourself through the following (or similar) thoughts: 'what day is it today? ... so yesterday was ... so we're talking about ... now, what was I doing on ...' and so on.

Maybe you asked yourself more questions, maybe fewer. You will have almost certainly arrived at the answer by connecting one thought with another. It's probably a question that no one else has asked you so far today, so you will have had to make the pathway to the answer for the *first time*. Had the question been 'what's your name?' or 'what instrument do you teach?' then, because you've made the pathway to those answers so many times, they would come popping into your brain immediately, without any further thinking. What we've discovered here is something very important – we've discovered how the brain likes to work. It's all to do with making connections and generating patterns of thought; connecting one piece of information with another.

This is, fundamentally, how we think. We connect one (easily recalled) thought with another (and another and another …) and finally we get to the answer – which might, for example, be a piece of information stored away deeply in some far recess of our mind. Or, by connecting one thought with another we may generate a completely new thought – a new idea, a new way of expressing something we've articulated in the same old way so many times before. It is through making connections that we begin to *understand*. The brain will naturally and subconsciously make sense of what we present it with, especially if we do so by making clear connections.

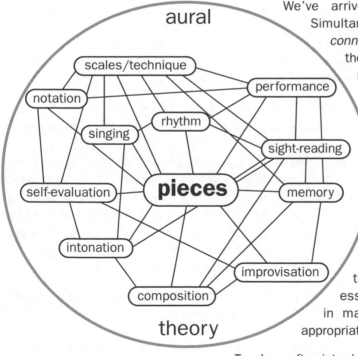

We've arrived at the first principle of Simultaneous Learning – *everything connects*. Have a look at the model on the left. It's not an entirely accurate representation because *everything* connects to *everything else*, but the point is clearly made.

'Pieces' are in the middle because they represent the core activity from where all our teaching should grow. By using pieces to stimulate thought and work on any area of musical activity, our pupils can really begin to understand the *relevance* of that work. The essence of teaching successfully is in making these connections clear, appropriate and comprehensible.

Teachers often introduce interesting activities and ideas into their lessons but today's 'streetwise' pupils can sometimes see these as random. And because they are often stand-alone activities they don't make any real sense. As soon as we make connections with the pieces, there is immediately a strong reason for making a detour to a scale or arpeggio, to aural or theory work, a musical 'game', or an improvisation.

You'll also notice that aural and theory seem to be 'floating' – that is because they must continually infuse our teaching.

As musicians we understand intuitively how all these connections work. If we're lucky, we might have one or two 'star' pupils who seem to do so too. However, the vast majority of our pupils need help to make these connections, in order to see how it all fits together and so begin to form their own understanding.

> **As we teach we must continually make these connections, explaining to our pupils exactly how one thing connects with another. This should form the very basis of our teaching.**

Spend some time thinking about these connections: choose some of the areas from the Simultaneous Learning model on the previous page and think about how they connect. For example, you might connect PIECES and SCALES: the piece is in the key of X, so pupils work at *that* particular scale and arpeggio. Then they discover where those patterns appear in the piece.

Now we might make a further connection with THEORY: pupils write down the key signature and the scale and arpeggio. Then we might make a connection with AURAL: reading from notation, pupils hear the scale and arpeggio internally. Or you might connect SIGHT-READING and SCALES: many sight-reading patterns are based on scale or arpeggio patterns – so pupils do some work on the appropriate scales and arpeggios from NOTATION (another connection) so that they easily recognise the patterns when sight-reading, which will encourage more fluency.

The number of connections is endless: everything connects.

When you're sitting in a traffic jam or waiting at a bus stop, think through more connections and how they might unfold in a lesson. We often have an intuitive understanding about these connections but we need to bring them into our conscious thinking too. As you teach, they will begin to pop into your mind as you're going along. Feel confident to change direction as they do, always remembering to explain carefully to your pupils what you're doing. The mind *needs* to make these connections to enable real understanding.

Here's an example of how we might introduce a practice sight-reading test into a lesson using the Simultaneous Learning process:

First of all choose a SIGHT-READING 'test' that reinforces a RHYTHM occurring in the PIECE being studied. Play some rhythm games to ensure that the rhythm is understood. Write that rhythm pattern down (THEORY). Hear it internally (AURAL). Make up a short tune using that rhythm pattern (IMPROVISATION).

Now hear the rhythm of the complete sight-reading piece internally (AURAL). Clap the rhythm. Play the SCALE of the sight-reading piece (perhaps using the rhythm if it fits) from NOTATION *and also* from MEMORY. Try to hear the rhythm and melodic shape of the sight-reading piece internally.

Look at the first bar or two again for a few moments, hearing them internally, then try to hear them from MEMORY. Finally, play the test. (We'll talk about whether this is really 'sight-reading' later on.)

In a short time we would have made connections from the piece to at least seven areas of our Simultaneous Learning model and we are teaching pupils to really *understand* every aspect of what they are doing. This is so much better than simply giving a pupil a practice sight-reading test which they will (more often than not) stumble and struggle their way through and feel positively de-motivated after having done so.

Instead of lessons trudging the same well-trodden path again and again (and again) a lesson can become a voyage of discovery with one thing leading naturally to another; musical connections being made as and when they come into your mind (or your pupil's mind), or as they simply materialise. It's an exciting prospect and a method of teaching that allows you to be more thorough – it reduces the likelihood of taking short cuts or teaching something without clear explanation. Each connection you make informs and clarifies the last and all learners (whether slow or fast) will benefit.

A number of teachers occasionally express a concern here: 'this kind of teaching takes *longer*'. Longer than what? We sometimes have this anxiety that if our teaching doesn't seem to be moving in a (seemingly) forward direction and at high speed all the time, then something is amiss. Teaching shouldn't be in a hurry – we don't have to get pupils through another exam every few months. Let's always have the confidence to teach thoroughly and broadly, which will mean that instead of giving up (as so many do), pupils will eventually have the understanding to make much more accelerated progress and become confident, independent learners.

Have you had the following (not uncommon) experience? I inherited an enthusiastic pupil who came to me announcing that he was grade seven standard. In fact the 'grade seven standard' was entirely artificial. His previous teacher had somehow taught him to play grade seven pieces but it was all an illusion as his technique and musical understanding were really around grade three. It took about three years to get him to a real grade seven standard. His enthusiasm and strong-mindedness got him through: it might not have done though and he may easily have lost interest and given up. It seemed to be an example of irresponsible teaching – connections had not been made. There were neither foundations nor understanding.

How's the hamster?

At the start of a lesson all teachers chat with their pupils. These are very valuable moments – making contact and showing we're interested helps that hugely important teacher-pupil relationship to develop. But what happens next? Does the lesson take on a compartmentalised kind of format; most of the time spent reacting to pupils playing through the current pieces, perhaps a scale or two (maybe from an exam syllabus but probably not in the same keys as the pieces played earlier)? Then a tiny snippet of unprepared sight-reading (of which the pupil makes a terrible mess) and finally (if there are a few minutes left), 'don't you have an exam next week? We'd better do some aural ...' I exaggerate, of course, but it does happen. Occasionally there is room for structured, compartmentalised teaching, however, it should be the exception rather than the rule (more on this later).

Together with compartmentalised teaching often comes the long-established system of modelling and correction. That is: show pupils how to do it, give them appropriate materials with which to practise and then correct them when they go wrong. In a sense there's nothing wrong with this kind of methodology. It's a fairly reasonable way of teaching and it has worked for a great many pupils over a great many years. But does it always produce the best results? Does it take into account the fact that:

- Pupils often learn at very different speeds?
- Many pupils gradually get ground down by the continual mistake/correction process?
- Many pupils may be more right- or left-brain dominant and so require different kinds of teaching? (More on this later too.)

In fact modelling is important – our pupils do need to be shown how to do it. They do need to hear a mature and well-produced tone quality, tone colour or dynamic and they do need to hear their teacher occasionally inspiring them with an exquisitely shaped phrase. (The importance of giving pupils well-chosen materials goes without saying.) It's the continual correction of mistakes that needs addressing and the fact that teachers often end up simply reacting to pupils' work (or lack of it), rather than setting the agenda.

'Bar one' teaching

The modelling-correction mode of teaching tends to encourage teachers and pupils to open their method books or put the current piece on the music stand, locate bar one and, irrespective of what's coming round the corner, set off bravely until the first mistake is made or the first hurdle causes a nasty fall. Let's think about this method for a moment.

Sally comes to her lesson after a week of (less than) average practice. In other words, a number (perhaps even all) of those problems that should have been put right, haven't been. Sally is already feeling a little anxious. Off we go from

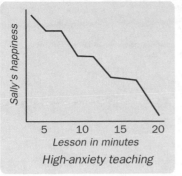

High-anxiety teaching

bar one; the first mistake is made and corrected. Sally feels a mixture of embarrassment at not having practised well enough (she's usually a well-intentioned pupil), chastised for making the mistake and tense because she's not sure whether she'll get it right second time around. She has another go but doesn't get it quite right … imagine how this might continue – it's not an uncommon scenario.

Let's consider Sally's feelings: even before the lesson has begun she is already a little anxious and at each stumble she becomes just a little more stressed, unsettled and unhappy. It's high-anxiety teaching – hardly ideal. A stressed pupil is not a happy pupil and will find it very difficult to learn.

This is the problem with what I call 'bar one' teaching, and although we need to begin at bar one from time to time, I'd like to suggest another approach that takes us to the second principle of Simultaneous Learning.

A couple of golden rules

Let's consider how you might teach the first lesson on a new piece. Golden rule number one:

Leave the notation out of sight – DON'T OPEN THE BOOK!

Instead, we're going to allow the lesson to unfold, based on the piece's *ingredients*. So golden rule number two, and the second principle of Simultaneous Learning, is:

Find and teach from a piece's *ingredients*

Here's an example:

I've got those 'I'm a great teacher' blues

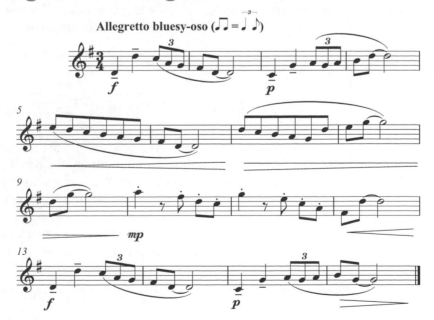

Here are the piece's main ingredients:

Key: G major

Time: 3/4

Important rhythmic pattern: ♩ ♩ ♫♩ | ♫ ♩ ♩ |

Rhythm: Swinging quavers

Dynamic markings: *f* *mp* *p*

Articulation markings: ♩ ♩

Character: Jazzy, laid-back, cool, relaxed, unconcerned.

Technical matters: playing with a smooth legato; crossing the middle register smoothly.

Instead of beginning at bar one, we're going to use some of these ingredients to make connections with aural work and concept development through musicianship activities and games, improvisation and memory work. Here's how a first lesson (individual or group) on the above piece might unfold:

You've set a 3/4 pulse going (perhaps coming quietly from a hidden metronome or by gently tapping your foot from the very moment pupils enter your room).

Begin with some warm-ups (still with that 3/4 pulse tapping away) and then (in 3/4) play some call-and-response[2] games – play two-bar phrases in G major and pupils play them back. Encourage pupils to listen carefully to tone quality and intonation.

Introduce the two extreme dynamics in our ingredient list, *f* and *p*. Then introduce a G major scale, a few notes at a time; play them swung with a lovely legato, then play them staccato. Use those two dynamics. Build up a whole octave if things are going well.

Next, introduce the rhythmic pattern, using call-and-response, perhaps through a simple phrase on G:

Perhaps play question-and-answer games with the rhythm. Pupils answer you with the same rhythm but change the notes (tell pupils which notes they are allowed to use). You might introduce some words to fit the rhythm (e.g. 'I like pineapple ice cream'). Pupils hear the rhythm internally and then combine that with clapping it. Then pupils write the rhythm down (pupils should often write some music down in lessons – see page 50). Now play the scale again in the *character* of the piece … and so on.

[2] Throughout this book 'call-and-response' work is where teacher plays and pupil repeats exactly; 'question-and-answer' is where teacher plays and pupil answers with a related but in some way altered response.

Teaching in this way will mean that you'll have to know the piece. If it's new to you too, a couple of minutes thinking through it and making a list of the main ingredients is all that it takes. If you do make a list, commit it to memory. Having to refer to a written list of ingredients during the lesson will spoil the flow.

This is Simultaneous Learning in action. Where the lesson goes will depend on how your pupils respond – it is a voyage of discovery. And of course, teaching in this way will provide you with many opportunities to praise. You might cover just a few of the ingredients in the first lesson or (depending on the pupil) many of them. Send pupils home to think about and absorb the ingredients, use them for improvising, play musical games. How you allow this to develop is very much up to you. Some teachers I know like to introduce the notation in the second lesson, others continue with this kind of work for two or more weeks. You may like to spend a few minutes on this kind of work – or the whole lesson. It's entirely up to you.

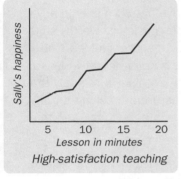

Sally's happiness

Lesson in minutes

High-satisfaction teaching

There will be other pieces at different stages of development but again always begin each piece with ingredient work first and open the music later. By teaching in this way you are virtually removing all that potential for anxiety. During those all-important first five or ten minutes of the lesson, where Sally's inner feelings could go one way or the other (which will affect the success of the whole lesson), you are ensuring that they can only go one way: in an *upward* direction. Spirits are raised, confidence increases and so teaching and learning will always be positive and effective.

The map is not the territory

However you begin your lessons, try to put the activity or material into an aural and/or memory context. In this way pupils are *being musical* from the start. Whilst notation work is of course very important, do remember that notes on a page are not music and a pupil struggling to read some half-understood notation is not enjoying a *musical* experience. That's why preparation, in the Simultaneous Learning manner, is so crucial – you are teaching, and your pupils are learning, in a real musical environment.

To play or not to play …

Should you play a new piece to your pupils? Some pupils benefit considerably from hearing the whole piece, all the ingredients in place, before they begin to learn it[3]. For others it doesn't matter. Vary your approach, sometimes giving pupils a performance and sometimes not.

The 'aha!' factor

When you do finally open the book with all this preparation having taken place, your pupils will look at the music and say, 'Oh yes! I understand that. It's in G major. There's that rhythmic pattern and here it is again. I can see the staccato and the dynamics, I know how that bit goes …' When they begin to play, they are less likely to forget the dynamics or the F sharps; there will be character

[3] Especially those who are more right-brain dominant (see more about this in Chapter 3).

too. They already have some real insight into the music; they already know a lot about it. It's so much more exciting than 'bar one' teaching – struggling through the piece, with pupils making the same old mistakes that you can virtually predict every time – and all the negative vibes that go with it.

As they are about to start work on a new piece with a pupil, I've had teachers say to me, 'I know all the mistakes this pupil is going to make'. The look of horror on my face always causes an interesting reaction. Pupils should be taught in such a way that will cause them rarely, if ever, to make mistakes – and if you know what the mistakes might be, then make sure the preparation is such that they *won't* make them!

Simultaneous Learning does exactly that – it prepares pupils so that they won't make mistakes – and because you're teaching in a much more thorough way, pupils are able to apply their knowledge. You won't have to teach the same thing over and over again – your pupils will have learnt *effectively*. You probably know the difference between a good lesson and an effective one. I've seen many a *good* lesson: teacher explains well and uses enjoyable music and worthy study books but at the end the pupil may not have done much successful learning. It may have been a *good* lesson – but not an *effective* one. An effective lesson is where pupils really understand, absorb and then are able to re-apply that understanding. That comes from making connections, from teaching through the ingredients, being really thorough, using appropriate language and thus being much more aware of your pupils' learning.

Additionally, because they are applying their knowledge and skill more reliably, your pupils will learn more quickly and you will be able to cover much more repertoire. We want to move well away from the kind of teaching that rigidly sticks to exam syllabuses, so that pupils learn only the exam pieces. In a worst-case scenario, a pupil having worked through all the grades may only have ever learnt twenty-four pieces and remained under the impression that the only point of scales is to get through an exam!

Getting from A to B: teachers as miracle makers

Much of what we do is to bring about that miraculous change whereby, through our effective teaching, pupils who can't do something find that eventually they can. Sometimes that change takes place very quickly; sometimes it takes many hours or even months of dedicated hard work. Sometimes it concerns technical matters; sometimes artistic. In helping our students to overcome any kind of challenge we must be able and prepared to present them with a whole host of short-, medium- and long-term strategies, drawing on our skills, knowledge, experience and especially our imagination.

Preferred learning styles

What do you feel when pupils can't do something, even after you've provided them with a superbly crystal clear set of instructions that seem to have worked on every other pupil you've ever taught? Do you feel frustrated, perhaps even slightly angry, or do you feel 'whoopee! Now I can really show what a good teacher I am'? I hope it's the latter – a pupil who can't do something is a real and exciting challenge. Patience, energy and imagination will eventually cause you to come up with the solution. Here's how.

Very occasionally we may simply say something so inspirational that it causes a 'eureka' moment and our pupil gets from A (can't do it) to B (can do it) almost instantaneously. More often it takes a bit more than that and we may have to create anything from two or three 'in-between' activities to perhaps many hundreds. If you think simultaneously, then these sequential connections will emerge with little effort and you will find yourself creating a progression of activities that will gradually build up the necessary ability. Perhaps (for a particular pupil) the answer to a problem lies in making connections with aural work through theory, or perhaps something will suddenly become clear through improvising a series of sequential exercises. Maybe the solution can be found by listening to someone else playing the same passage, by expressing the idea using different language, or through making connections with particularly vivid images.

The secret is to approach the problem from as many different angles as possible – teaching the same thing in lots of different ways is to teach powerfully. Here knowledge of 'preferred learning styles' is useful. If you look up preferred learning styles on the internet you will probably find more than one set. I find the most straightforward and comprehensible is the division into visual, auditory and kinaesthetic (which indicates a hands-on, practical approach).

When you buy a new piece of electronic gadgetry do you read the manual, ask a friend how to work it or fiddle around until it starts doing whatever it should? Which is your preferred learning style? In fact we all learn using all three styles in some proportion and the style of learning may not always be the same for each task we undertake. We may prefer one style of learning for one task and a combination of others for another task. Our pupils are just the same. Nevertheless, in general:

Visual learners prefer:
- Working from notation
- Reading explanations of technical matters
- Sight-reading
- Looking at other visual stimuli (e.g. pictures that may suggest musical character, diagrams that may explain technical areas)
- Written (theory) work

Auditory learners prefer:
- Aural work
- Call-and-response activities
- Verbal explanations
- Discussion
- Talking
- Musical demonstrations with discussion

Kinaesthetic learners prefer:
- Copying and experimenting
- Call-and-response activities
- Improvising and composing
- Asking questions
- Writing

As you can see already, styles overlap. It's not in any way necessary (or indeed especially helpful) for you to determine the precise preferred learning style of each of your pupils, though you probably will notice one is more dominant in most. What we can usefully learn from this is the number of teaching strategies available. Whatever you teach, try to make connections with each learning style if possible. The more ways we teach the same thing, the more powerful the learning.

For example, say you are working on a technically awkward passage from a new piece. You might go through the following series of activities:

Begin by analysing exactly what the problem is, then build up an aural picture of the phrase with some call-and-response work based on fragmenting and/or simplifying the original.

Analyse the pattern (is it based on some scale or arpeggio pattern?); play those patterns; hear the pattern internally; write down the pattern; transpose the pattern (or fragments of it) into different keys.

As part of practice, pupils then improvise or compose their own exercises to help further.

In this way you have used visual (writing, analysing), auditory (call-and-response, transposing, internalisation) and kinaesthetic (writing, improvising, composing) strategies through making Simultaneous Learning connections, which have taken your pupil to many of those musical areas. This is thorough teaching.

Occasionally pupils may still not get it. There's no shame in putting the problem on the back burner for a while and returning to it later – work on other related areas in the meantime. When you return to the original problem it may well have gone some way to sorting itself out.

Never having to say 'no'

What about that pupil who does need lots of those 'in-between' activities? What do you say when they fail to grasp it for the twenty-fifth time? 'No, not like that.' 'No, that's not it.' 'No, do it like this!'. 'No! No! No! No! No!'

'No' is one of those dispiriting words that we ought to use rarely. I well remember a teacher who often used the word 'no'– his pupils were not happy. 'No' rarely elicits positive feelings; usually pupils are more likely to feel belittled, stupid, ashamed, nervous and even angry. One of the great advantages of Simultaneous Learning is that you are always looking for new ways to overcome problems. So, if a pupil can't do something, or gets it wrong, don't say 'no' but instead, 'nearly, let's try this …'

Save 'no' for those advanced pupils who can take it and (occasionally) need a tougher approach!

Don't expect overnight results

If you feel you'd like to absorb some of these ideas into your teaching (you probably already use many of them) then it's best to do so gradually. Pupils who expect the bar one approach will take a little time to adjust but the results will come and they can be quite spectacular. Many pupils will find this kind of teaching both exciting and exhilarating: they will understand exactly what you're up to very quickly and will respond with great enthusiasm. Others will take time to modify their ways but after a while will begin to get much more out of it. The benefits for you can be far-reaching – teaching suddenly becomes much more active, stimulating and exciting. You're not sitting (or standing) there simply reacting to and then correcting your pupils' errors, which is guaranteed to produce boredom and low spirits in both parties. Your mind is always alert, driving the lesson in ever new and interesting directions. Teaching has become a voyage of discovery.

The teaching continuum

Of course there will be times – an approaching exam for example – when you will need to teach in a compartmentalised kind of way. There will also be times when you will want to spend a lot of time in very detailed study; the whole lesson spent on a scale (or part of it), the first subject (or indeed note!) of a Mozart or Brahms sonata, some aspect of posture, or the shaping of some glorious phrase. The result is the Simultaneous Learning *sliding scale* – an infinite continuum of lesson styles that is tremendously liberating, for it means that every lesson can be taught differently.

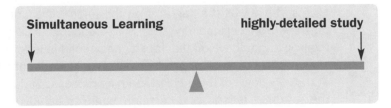

You may wish to give a completely 'organic' Simultaneous Learning type of lesson where, based on a piece or pieces, one musical activity simply leads to another and another and another. The lesson seems naturally to unfold, teacher and pupil responding to each other: a feast for the imagination. Or you may wish to spend the whole lesson on some finer point of technique or interpretation (which many pupils love doing, particularly as they become more advanced), which is equally invigorating and challenging in a different way.

In between the two extremes you have an unlimited range of lesson types – part simultaneous, part detailed work – dependent on all sorts of factors: an imminent concert performance at school or in a festival, a pupil has forgotten to bring any music, the weather, only half the group has turned up, a pupil has a new hamster (or a new instrument), has to learn a part for the school orchestra, is tired, is very late, has just come from a difficult maths lesson ... Whatever the situation, you should feel armed and confident to provide effective teaching in any eventuality!

Plan to prepare

I'm often asked how much *planning* should go into a lesson. There are usually too many variables and unforeseeable conditions to 'plan' *each lesson* in too much detail. However it is important to plan your short-, medium- and long-term objectives: it is essential to know, in general terms, where each pupil is going. The teaching of general musical concepts, repertoire, technical work, exams, festivals and other performance opportunities begin to connect and form a broad curriculum. Particular objectives over half a term, for example, would fit the medium-term (perhaps specific repertoire and technical work) and working for an exam or a general overview of a year's work would fit the long-term. It is certainly very important to *prepare* each lesson. Know what pupils are supposed to be practising and have a general idea of the direction in which you wish the lesson to go but remember that the imagination must always be allowed to flourish. Don't worry if the lesson occasionally does end up going in an entirely different direction to that which you planned.

Simultaneous Learning for the advanced pupil

The processes of Simultaneous Learning will work just as effectively for your more advanced pupils. Again I must repeat that this is not a new teaching method – the ideas, strategies and teaching concepts are already very much the domain of many skilful, thoughtful and imaginative teachers. I am simply drawing these thoughts and strategies together in a more formalised way.

I am sure we would all agree that the underlying function of all good music teaching (from beginner onwards) is to broaden and deepen our pupils' musical thinking and to develop their ability and confidence to make informed choices in all aspects of musical development. This leads to the understanding that lies at the very heart of the musical learning process. Simultaneous Learning, from the very first lesson, will certainly begin to achieve these ends. As pupils progress, more areas of learning enter the arena and begin to play a more central and demanding role, so in addition to further development of aural, key-sense, scales, technique, theory, rhythm and sight-reading (and all their various relations), we start to see the gradual emergence of practical analysis, stylistic conventions, historical context, harmony and the growing need to develop the pupils' ability to mould their *own* interpretation.

Perhaps you might now like to repeat the exercise we did at the beginning of this chapter. Make a list of all the elements of music teaching – this time including all the 'new' areas (both those I have suggested and any others that may occur to you) and make two or three connections between each of them. As you teach, you will continually see more and more vistas opening up and increasingly more imaginative routes down which to guide your pupils.

As our experience grows, we soon begin to recognise (even among our very elementary pupils) those who will go on to take music seriously, passing through to the high grades and perhaps even further. Of course, as teachers of integrity, we aim to deliver the same quality of teaching to all our pupils but human nature and background will cause some pupils to shine more despite our efforts. These pupils will be more likely to go to concerts and actively listen to music. As we begin to detect a real glimmer of enthusiasm, we should encourage them to build a collection of recordings of music they will eventually play. These 'broadening' activities will bring about many advantages: pupils will begin to develop their own *internal perception* of the sound world and potential of their instrument or voice; they will *know* that Bach, Mozart, Beethoven, Shostakovich or Gershwin piece prior to learning it – perhaps even for a number of years. It will have become part of their experience. 'But they'll play it just like Murray Perahia' is a comment occasionally thrown back at me. My answer is simply, 'if only ...'

The sum total of their own musical experiences, the potential of *their* ear and technique will of course produce a performance quite different from Maestro Perahia's but what they would have learnt by knowing his, and hopefully other, interpretations will be considerable. Of course we also need to be able to teach pupils to learn entirely unknown music, which is all part of helping our pupils to become independent learners. Let's consider, for example, how we might set about teaching a new work to a grade eight or advanced pupil.

Teaching a big sonata movement

Let us take a big sonata movement. In many ways, learning a new piece of music is like learning a part in a play – it is always both fascinating and illuminating listening to a great actor talking about a big role. He or she will have thought deeply about it. Similarly, pupils need to know their music deeply, building up a personal and profound 'relationship' with the piece – both during practice and performance. Great music deserves serious study – what actor would approach roles like Hamlet or King Lear, Lady Macbeth or Ophelia, in a cavalier fashion?

Pupils should listen intelligently to the music. They must begin to develop ideas about the piece: what does it mean emotionally? What is the music saying? What does it mean to *them*? They must use their discerning ear to understand exactly what is going on – this is making real connections with aural perception. Make connections with 'practical' analysis as well: yes, it *is* necessary to understand the overall structure of the movement but pupils should also understand how melodic ideas unfold, develop and connect, how rhythmic patterns inhabit different melodic guises and perhaps how the composer develops the music within both varying textures and sonorities. What is the significance of similar phrases sometimes ascending, sometimes descending?

Once pupils have developed some understanding of the music, make time to discuss the style and make connections with the historical context too. As a result, they will begin to develop their own personal approach to the music and they are well on the way to a performance of real musical insight.

More ingredients

Then, identify the ingredients just as we did with our simple pieces but now looking for more sophisticated ones. Think about the technical, stylistic and musical ideas that add up to make the whole. These may lead to improvisations – to develop and overcome a technical problem perhaps, or to assimilate a point of style. Work out the various keys through which the music travels and work at the scales and their related patterns *in association* with the music, not as unconnected, technical exercises in a few moments at the beginning or end of the lesson (or practice). Encourage your pupils to listen to other works by the same composer. Play the scales and other patterns in the style of the composer.

Towards an interpretation

A number of weeks may have passed by now and we still might not have begun to play the piece through from bar one. Our work so far has been directed towards building up a 'concept' of the music, acquiring a deep knowledge of its content and meaning. Our pupils will have identified – and perhaps learnt and memorised – the technically demanding passages. They will have listened to and made connections with other works by the composer in order to broaden their understanding. Together you will have spent some quality time talking about the music. So now we come to putting it all together and developing an interpretation. Again we must remember the underlying philosophy of Simultaneous Learning: to continually draw and make connections with a wide range of musical and imaginative thinking and to keep our minds open.

As far as possible, encourage pupils to take ownership of their interpretation. Aural activity remains the central source of developing an interpretation. There is of course no definitively right or correct way to play any piece and it is never our job to tell our pupils definitively how something should 'go'. We should encourage pupils to use their ears to experiment and discover different solutions to each musical challenge and then through questions and discussion we ultimately lead them into making their decision (perhaps with a little appropriate guidance). This decision may not, of course, be final. By virtue of working in this way we broaden the range of possibilities and in performance their musical imaginations might take them to a completely new but equally meaningful negotiation of a particular musical 'corner'.

Independent learning

By teaching in this broader and more holistic manner, we have taught our pupils not simply to play this sonata movement but, much more importantly, how to approach music of this calibre. In so doing, we have given them the necessary ability and confidence to learn other sonatas *on their own*.

When using Simultaneous Learning with our younger and less advanced pupils, this approach may take a little more thought, more preparation and more time but the rewards are much richer. We are teaching our pupils to think musically and to think for themselves. We are not simply teaching them 'the instrument' or 'the piece'; we are teaching them to become artists and we are giving them the confidence to develop their own insights into great art.

3 Left and right

We hear a lot about the left and right hemispheres of the brain these days and a modest knowledge of this very fascinating subject can help us considerably in our teaching. So, let's explore a little and have a look at what each side of our brain is doing.

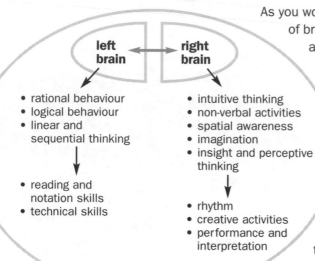

left brain
- rational behaviour
- logical behaviour
- linear and sequential thinking

- reading and notation skills
- technical skills

right brain
- intuitive thinking
- non-verbal activities
- spatial awareness
- imagination
- insight and perceptive thinking

- rhythm
- creative activities
- performance and interpretation

As you would expect, the actual scientific reality of brain function is rather complex. It is not a simple case of black and white. However, over the years, a considerable body of scientific evidence to support 'right' and 'left' functions of the brain has emerged and certainly the concept of right/left is a very useful (metaphorical) model for understanding the way we think.

The left side, musically speaking, is in charge of reading and technique. A number of teachers seem to draw only on this side of the brain. Their pupils can develop good (sometimes excellent) techniques and will be able to read music confidently and accurately. Performances by such pupils may have some connection with what the composer intended but they are missing something very important. They are missing the areas that are stimulated by the right brain, which are essential in completing the picture. The right side of the brain is where the imagination lives and so it controls all matters creative – most notably interpretation, performance and composition.

A great many teachers are generally happy about the ways and means of teaching the left-brain work but the areas controlled by the right brain sometimes cause hesitation, doubt and uncertainty. Let's have a close look to alleviate any such feelings once and for all and start to place right-brain work where it should be – at the centre of our teaching.

As far as instrumental or singing teaching is concerned, the right brain is in charge of three main areas of musical activity: aural, memory and improvisation. Let's look at each in turn.

Aural

Aural (and I don't mean aural tests) is all about being able to hear or see music, then process and understand it *internally* – in the musical mind, through the musical ear. It is about making listening an *active* process. Aural tests are just a small branch, which, if we are constantly making connections with *aural* (in the larger sense of the word), should become easily understandable and manageable.

I've heard teachers say that they 'don't teach aural', or 'we only do aural when there's an exam coming up'. In fact, aural is at the very heart of being a musician and all lessons should begin with some kind of aural work. Not only does this have the advantage of creating an atmosphere where anxiety and tension are much less likely to thrive but it also turns on the right brain and makes a direct link with the imagination. By continually making connections with aural, pupils will improve their playing and singing enormously as well as becoming much more musically intelligent and perceptive. Aural develops sensitivity to quality and control of tone; improves sight-reading; helps pupils develop the ability to spot their own mistakes; develops sensitivity to others when playing or singing in an ensemble; improves awareness of intonation; improves ability to memorise, improvise and compose; develops an understanding of musical structure and language; and will help pupils to play more stylistically and develop a greater depth of expression. This last connection is very important – we don't always make it.

> **Think of one of your favourite pieces. Now hear it in your head with the most exquisite tone quality and phrasing.**

When pupils of mine have played a new phrase a few times I'll ask them to hear it in their head as *expressively as they can*. I then ask them to try and play it in the same way. Expressive shaping has to come from somewhere and that somewhere should be our own musical ears, our musical mind, our musical imagination – call it what you will. I could say to my pupils 'play it like this' or instruct them to listen to my favourite recording but that's not teaching them to develop their own ability to generate musical shaping from within their own musical minds.

The next stage is to ask pupils to play it from memory – the second of the three right-brain areas.

Memory

Even if you never ask or expect pupils to perform from memory, there should always be some memory work in lessons. Whatever the piece, and however long pupils have been learning it, they will be able to play somewhere between the first note and the whole piece from memory. If it's just the first note, then you can work at tone quality and colour, and character. Can you infuse the character of the piece into the first note? It's certainly worth a try! If they know more, then tossing phrases back and forth between you and your pupils is great fun. 'Try it this way ... or this ... how else could we shape this phrase?' It's surprising and very stimulating just how much you can do once you are liberated from the notation.

Memory work near the start of the lesson also helps to focus your pupil's concentration. Playing a short phrase (eyes closed) from memory will often help to focus the most boisterous and hyperactive twelve-year-old. On a more practical note, if pupils don't want to learn the whole piece from memory, then the least they should do is learn the 'black bits' from memory – those sections where there seem to be a rather daunting number of notes per square centimetre. When it comes to performance, anxiety is much reduced because pupils know that they *know* those tricky passages.

Memory work, of course, further develops the ear, for not only is the music being generated by the 'musical ear' but the 'hearing ear' can then go on to refine and polish what it hears. Playing 'by ear' leads us to the third and certainly the most provocative of the right-brain activities …

Improvisation

Improvisation is one of those musical activities that people seem to either love or hate. For some it strikes terror into their very hearts; others embrace it as though it were the most natural thing in the world. In fact it's a very useful teaching tool (and I am not thinking of jazz, or of improvising a set of variations, a sonata movement or fugue but something much more practical). Picture the following scenario:

> To pupil: 'I'd like you to improvise a piece that uses the following musical ingredients. It's going to be in C major, about *mf* and I'd like you to include some staccato.'
>
> Here's the response:
>
>
>
> Your reaction: 'First class … short but it hit the nail on the head. Perhaps we could try a longer one now, say two notes?'

Suddenly improvisation becomes manageable and non-threatening. This is what I call 'practical improvisation'– simply using improvisation to help pupils understand and experiment with musical ideas and concepts. It is an invaluable tool and you should use it from lesson one with all pupils. If you do, pupils will always be happy to improvise, play by ear, memorise and generally be creative without being self-conscious or coy. Whenever you teach something new or wish to reinforce or revisit *anything*, use improvisation. Pupils will feel quite happy making up short phrases to indicate that they've understood something, making up short exercises to help overcome a technical problem, or making up little tunes in the style of the piece they are learning – the applications are endless. If you are presently suspicious of improvisation, try it out – you're just a small step away from opening up a whole new world of possibilities in your teaching.

The advantages of bringing improvisation into your daily work are many: it is yet another activity that further develops the ear; it develops musical awareness (through playing around with ingredients); it develops creative thinking and sensitivity; it develops the part of the brain which solves problems; it develops thinking speed (very important for all musicians); it develops confidence; and it helps to reduce reliance on notation. Pupils won't simply freeze if there are no notes to hide behind.

Improvisation also has an important effect on conventional performance. The greatest performances have a certain improvisatory feel about them, as though the performer is playing the piece for the first time – there is a sense of spontaneity. Pupils who are brought up with improvisation in their diet will naturally bring a more creative approach to their playing.

Doing it the 'right' way

These three enormously important right-brain activities (aural, memory and improvisation) all draw upon and excite the imagination and they form a *permanent source from which all our teaching should flow.*

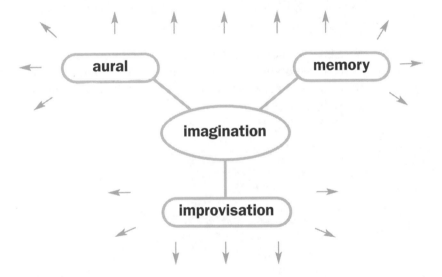

This constant right-brain work, together with continually making connections, will begin to cause our pupils to *think musically*. I don't mean thinking *about* music – thinking about the piece or the composer and so on – I mean thinking like we do, thinking like a musician; intuitively beginning to understand how it all fits together. It's very exciting when it begins to happen – you'll be able to detect it perhaps by a pupil suddenly showing concern for tone quality, or playing a phrase particularly artistically, with a shape you didn't suggest, or simply by making a musical comment or observation.

Extending choice

Think back to your own early teachers. Were you their star pupil? Probably. You were musically bright, making those connections, firing on both sides of the brain. To what extent do you copy your own teachers now as a teacher yourself?

You probably went down the fairly traditional route of learning from notation, taking and passing exams, doing well in festivals, going to university or music college. Some of your pupils will be just like you: fairly straightforward and rewarding to teach. But we must also be prepared to extend our gifts as teachers to those who may learn in different ways. What do you do with pupils who simply don't seem able, despite our very best efforts, to translate those symbols on the page to the appropriate physical responses?

I sat through an inspiring violin lesson once. It could have ended in disaster but the flexibility and imagination of the teacher won through. Malcolm, aged about seven, reluctantly came to his first lesson with this new teacher. The last had given him up as hopeless – he was simply never going to be able to read the notes. The new teacher worked for a while (from notation) on a piece that used just the open strings. Things were not going well. So instead of pursuing this route, together they invented a story. Each of the strings took the part of a different character in the story. And so the story unfolded … young Malcolm had a great time improvising and making sounds on his violin that perhaps would make some shudder but others positively relish. He decided that playing the violin was okay after all and back he came for more lessons. It was another six months before the teacher re-introduced some notation work again, by which time Malcolm was ready for it and determined to have a go.

We all need to be prepared to be flexible in our approach; to teach each pupil on their own merit: to unlock the treasure trove that lies in the right side of the brain. Otherwise we might lose many Malcolms along the way – and that is distinctly unfair!

4 Using the right brain

Many teachers are so comfortable with working on left-brain activities (such as teaching all aspects of technique and working with notation) that often the more exotic areas, under right-brain control, get sidelined. Indeed, some teachers are understandably a little unsure about quite how to tap into these right-brain areas, so they don't.

Clearly, without right-brain work we are only accessing half of the brain's potential – we are only teaching half of the pupil. We are simply teaching our pupils to operate their instruments, leaving any expressive, creative or imaginative qualities (or in other words *musical* qualities) to chance, luck or divine intervention. This need not be. In this chapter we'll see that right-brain work is simple to access and how it will considerably affect and expand our own minds as well as allowing us to teach in much greater depth.

How do we get there? How can we set up the appropriate conditions to allow access into the marvels of right-brain work? I hope the three main right-brain areas (aural, memory and improvisation) are now clearly flagged up in your mind. Working in any of those areas will turn the right brain on and once it's on we need to cultivate, nurture and develop it. We can then really begin to teach our pupils to be expressive – to play really musically. We've all met children who seem on the surface to be (in varying degrees) 'unmusical'. In fact, very few children are unmusical. For some, however, (be it because of background or psychological make-up, for example) cajoling that music out of them may be quite a challenge. So let's be positive and accept that we all have musical potential – it's just a case of finding it.

Look! It's a bird ... it's a plane ... no ... it's the left brain!

The left brain *is* a bit like Superman – it wants to do all the jobs. Left to its own devices it probably will, leaving the right brain idly looking on with interest but not being allowed to participate actively. The way to turn on the right side of the brain is to present it with a challenge that will cause the left side to say 'Okay – I concede that that's a job for my assistant, right brain!' We can do this by presenting the challenge *imaginatively*, because the imagination lives in the right side of the brain. Perhaps you're teaching a wind, brass or string instrument, or singing, and you're going to begin with some 'long note' work to warm up the tone-controlling apparatus. If you start with 'now I want you to play a long note – make sure that your rectus abdominus is exerting even all-round pressure and that your orbicularis oris balances that pressure equally', then of course you've blown it (literally, but also metaphorically!). Even if you were to say 'play a long note with an even tone', again the left brain is more likely to take on the job.

The key is presenting the challenge *imaginatively*. 'Can you play a long note with a mellow, deep blue colour, as if you were standing at the bottom of the

Grand Canyon?' That's a job the right brain will positively jump at. After pupils have had a go, you can then activate the left brain and tidy it up with some technical help but, in general, the rule is: from right to left. Present the challenge in such a way that the right side has first go.

This leads us on to the first of the two 'teaching with the right brain' principles: *the importance of vocabulary* i.e. the words we use to get across what we mean or what we want our pupils to do.

Watch what you say

Think about how you put things and try to remember the following two points:

One – that most of our pupils have much less experience of language than we do. Often we use sentence constructions that are just too complicated. Listen to what you're saying – is it crystal clear? Are you saying what you mean? Are you making assumptions? Are you being interesting? (Are you being succinct? Some teachers talk too much!)

Two – that most of our pupils have bigger and more interesting vocabularies than we might expect.

Is it 'happy' or 'sad'?

Yes, these are the two most often-used words in describing musical character but what dull words they are. Pupils simply switch off when they hear them. They have little meaning – they've been heard too many times before and don't excite the imagination. 'Happy' and 'sad' are fine as starters but we need to broaden our vocabulary – have a look at some children's books and you might be surprised at the kind of words you'll find, even in books for six- and seven-year-olds. Make lists – how many different (and more colourful) words can you find to develop 'happy' and 'sad'? Start to tap into your pupils' imaginations for vocabulary when you are discussing music. Ask them how *they* would describe the music.

The second principle

Think of a favourite piece of yours. Hear a section of it in your head and now ask yourself (and answer) the following questions:

> • What does it make me feel?
> • What does it make me think of?
> • Does it remind me of something – a place, a person, a special moment?
> • What's it like?

[4] Scholars of the English language will recognise that I'm using the word metaphor slightly loosely: here it incorporates simile and comparison too.

We've arrived at the second 'teaching with the right brain' principle: *the importance of metaphor* i.e. *this* is like *that* [4].

Metaphor is an essential tool in teaching because it can help us when taking our pupils on those journeys into unknown territory. Here we come back to that first principle of Simultaneous Learning – making connections. As we move into a new area (a skill, a concept, an idea, a character) we must connect it with something familiar. It is particularly important when dealing with musical character because we are asking our pupils to apply abstract thinking (character and expression) to a physical activity (playing the instrument) and that can be very mystifying.

Here are some 'metaphors' for you to think about: comparisons, images, similes, allegories, figures of speech … I'm sure you will already use a number of them and you will probably have favourites of your own. Pick and choose as you will. The kind of metaphors you use will be dependent on a pupil's age, nature and interests; the dynamics of the group; your own interests; the weather; what was on television last night. The list is endless.

Let's begin by thinking about how we can encourage a pupil into giving a really special performance.

Can we define that 'X' factor?

One of the great things about the art of musical performance is that anyone from virtual beginner, through grade five, grade eight, diploma, to great concert virtuoso can give a masterful performance – the kind of performance that has that tingle factor, that sends a shiver down our spine, that makes us sit up and take note. When it happens it's probably the result of the music being played:

- With character
- With involvement
- With meaning
- With intensity

It can be done, ultimately, by anyone at any age and at any level but it won't happen (except in very few cases) without a lot of help from us. How can we help pupils to begin to move towards that 'X' factor?

To be or not to be? That is the question

Most of our pupils will probably have been in a school play, or if not they will know what actors do through watching television or going to the cinema. Spend a few moments chatting about acting with your pupils.

If you're going to play a part you need to know the CHARACTER by understanding the kind of person he/she is, by understanding the kind of feelings and emotions he/she is experiencing and by understanding how the character interacts with others.

If you want to play that part a little more vividly then you begin to become interested in that character (perhaps exploring the character's background). That creates a real desire to bring the character to life, which brings about an INVOLVEMENT in the way the part is played. You become emotionally involved, really caring about (or understanding) the character.

You will want to know the MEANING of what the character is saying and find a way of delivering the lines to communicate that meaning. That will eventually lead you to a desire to communicate the character with a real and vivid INTENSITY.

It becomes instantly obvious that these are precisely the same factors that are necessary to produce a great musical performance.

Have you heard the one about … ?

'What did one hat say to the other hat?'
'You stay here. I'll go on ahead!'

The joke may or may not have made you groan, however, it certainly would have elicited some reaction – at least a gentle grin and a chuckle! Jokes are something all children know about and can relate to. So, why do we tell jokes?

- We enjoy making people laugh
- We enjoy sharing the fun
- We enjoy the reaction our joke-telling creates
- We enjoy being the centre of attention

I'm sure you can see the connection with giving a performance straight away and so will your pupils. Though, of course, the intention of a particular piece may be to make them cry rather than laugh, it's a great way to begin enticing those more stubborn pupils who think playing in public really isn't for them: performing really is just like telling a joke.

Tell me a story

We all enjoy a good story – whether it's a book, television drama, film, or listening to a skilled raconteur – and our young pupils love hearing and telling stories too. All pieces of music can tell a story, even if sometimes they don't seem to. Use your imagination, or draw out ideas from all your pupils – even from your older or more advanced pupils playing their more sophisticated pieces (some of whom may be a little reticent or even embarrassed about using their imagination so openly). No one is above storytelling and a sense of narrative is one of the most crucial ingredients in creating a cohesive performance. Some pieces will seem to present a clear narrative without too much trouble at all: titles like 'The penguins take a stroll' or 'Midnight on the River Moskva' will easily conjure up clear and vivid scenarios. 'Allegretto in F' may require a little more imagination but there's a story in there somewhere!

Music as a state of movement

All music lives at some point on a continuum of movement, somewhere between total inactivity and moving at the speed of light (metaphorically speaking). Use interesting images to stimulate ideas on how a piece should move. Try to think of some pieces you know and teach that fit the following images of movement:

- SLEEPING
- GRAZING like sheep
- Swans GLIDING over still water
- FIRING on all cylinders
- ZOOMING at the speed of light

Sometimes pupils find the concept of a *rallentando* hard to grasp. Try asking them to read a passage out loud with a *rall.* at the end of each sentence, or walk round in a circle, gradually slowing down. 'Real life' metaphors can be very effective.

Music as an expression of feeling

Music can of course express a feeling or state of mind. There is a continuum of emotion that runs from total contentment to utter anger. Let's look at the physical signs of feelings.

Contentment could be sitting, motionless, breathing gently, by a babbling brook on a warm sunny day watching the occasional cloud sail by. Or it could be watching your football team score the winning goal, where the outward display would be rather different! Anger could be stamping feet, wagging an admonitory finger, shouting with lots of emphatic gestures and so on. Thinking about the physical signs of feelings or states of mind is where we can make the connection with music.

This time, try to think of some pieces you play or teach that fit the following expressions of feeling:

- Warmly CONTENT by a cosy glowing coal fire
- ECSTATIC after your team has won the match
- DISTRAUGHT after losing something important
- ANGER between two rival groups

Places ... smells ... textures ... tastes ... shapes ...

Certain pieces may conjure up the sights, sounds, smells and atmosphere of a particular place, country or region. For example, if your pupil is learning 'Spanish fiesta!' then bring to the lesson some pictures of feasting and celebrating, dancing with castanets, sun and colourful costumes, and so on.

Textures might open the mind to some interesting sounds, from coarse or rough to silky or velvety. Food (textures and tastes) can suggest a multitude of ideas, from skimmed milk to thick double cream or yoghurt; from a piece of overcooked tough shoe-leather beef to a slice of lightly grilled salmon that melts in your mouth. From rich chocolate fudge cake to a crisp raw carrot. A phrase ending could be sweet or sour, bitter or tart. Children love food metaphors! Could you, perhaps, think of any pieces that suggest particular foods?

Shapes are very useful too – from the languorous curves of Chopin to the jagged edges of Bartók. They are also useful for thinking about sound. How might you use these three shapes to suggest different kinds of articulation, for example?

One particularly imaginative teacher told me that she always brings something that has an interesting texture or feel into each lesson to stimulate thinking about sounds – a balloon, a mirror, a hairbrush, a pineapple ...

Metaphors with drawing

Colour, contrasts, light and shade are all very useful concepts to apply, especially to sound. We often speak of tone *colour* – why not try out different colours? What colour do you see the opening of the slow movement from a favourite sonata or concerto, for example? We often speak of a dark or bright tone. A sound could be dense or transparent. A phrase could be in glorious sunshine or under ominous storm clouds.

Some pupils may like to paint or draw. Ask them to bring some of their work to the lesson – it could stimulate all kinds of interesting musical thought.

Language and speech

There are many useful parallels to be drawn from sentence structure and punctuation – we've all used punctuation to help teach cadences, for example. Think about the way we shape a spoken sentence, the way we 'phrase' words to give them meaning and the way we breathe when speaking to help pupils in their understanding of musical *flow*. Try talking about word emphasis to help introduce the very complex world of phrasing. You may well have your own favourite sentence to play this game but here's one if you don't. By placing a slight emphasis on a different word in the following sentence we can subtly alter its meaning:

- **I'm** going out tonight …   you can do as you please but that's what I'm doing.
- I'm **going** out tonight …   that's what I'm doing; I'm not staying in.
- I'm going **out** tonight …   not to sleep, not next door, just out!
- I'm going **to**night …   and no one is going to stop me!
- I'm going to**night** …   not this afternoon, not now, but tonight.

In the same way, part of the art of shaping a phrase is putting an emphasis on a particular note to give it a special meaning. Though shifting the emphasis does not significantly alter the meaning of the phrase, nevertheless there is a clear message in each version. We can even use this example to explain that there are sometimes occasions where an emphasis makes no sense and is best avoided:

- I'm go-**ing** out tonight

Then there are poetic metaphors, if your mind moves in this kind of way: 'play that phrase like the sun is rising over a glistening field of awakening, unfurling buttercups', or perhaps 'this movement is one continual attempt to swat a fly'.

The power of images and situations

Images and situations can be very powerful – choose them carefully and appropriately for each pupil. Use humour where you can, although it is worth remembering that dark images can create some wonderfully expressive and moving playing. I well remember a lesson with the great Karl Leister in which he described the end of the first movement of Brahms' *Clarinet Sonata in F minor* as 'an angel singing, welcoming you into heaven' – a powerful and unforgettable image. One could hardly play those bars inexpressively with that idea going through one's mind.

Put your pupil into situations: 'when you begin this piece, imagine you're …

- … setting off to a football match
- … an astronaut launching into outer space
- … Superman going to save the world
- … falling in love
- … waking up from a deep sleep

As soon as the imagination is engaged, the difference in what you'll hear will be very striking.

Technical problems can often be made very clear through sporting metaphors. I often teach my pupils to think of *backswing* in tennis or golf to help them achieve a better finger movement in legato playing.

Metaphors in practice

Let's look at one or two examples of how you might talk about some musical concepts through metaphor.

For those pupils who continually refuse to put any dynamic colour into their performance, we need to talk about the importance of contrast in life. It would all be a bit dull if there were always day and never night, if all food was savoury and nothing sweet. Large and small, heavy and light, on and off, high and low – all these contrasts help to give variety, interest, appeal and fascination to life. In music we must have loud and soft (or quiet if you prefer).

We must have dynamic contrasts in our performances. When f or p appear perhaps try one, or a combination, of the following thoughts – or something similar of your own (rather than 'you didn't do the *forte*!').

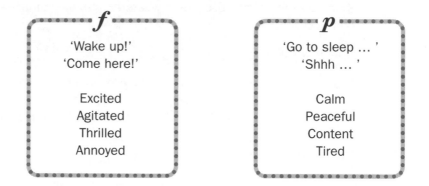

f

'Wake up!'
'Come here!'

Excited
Agitated
Thrilled
Annoyed

p

'Go to sleep ... '
'Shhh ... '

Calm
Peaceful
Content
Tired

'I didn't like scales either but you've got to learn them ... '

Just as there is a visual, auditory and kinaesthetic way of teaching pieces, we can also approach any musical activity in both a left- and right-brained way. Let's look, for instance, at the way we teach scales. Don't be like an otherwise very good teacher I knew, who would always send his pupils away to learn their scales by themselves – 'that's the way I was taught ... and I didn't like them either!' he would say. Scales need a lot of tender loving care and you must put imagination into the way you teach them. Only then will pupils begin to respond to (and practise) them without resentment.

Scales are neither hard nor boring but it's very much up to us, and the way that we present them, to ensure that they are not. Here are two sets of teaching strategies – one for the left brain and one for the right. Some pupils will naturally favour method and logic (left brain), others will prefer more fun-type activities (right brain). Use both – a good teacher will always be mixing and matching. You will also find the activities connect with many areas from our original Simultaneous Learning model.

Right-brain activities

- Teaching a pupil to hear a scale internally.
- Singing scale patterns (anything from two or three notes to a full octave).
- Learning scales from memory.
- Teacher playing a scale with a deliberate wrong note; pupil identifying it.
- Improvising/composing in the key using scale patterns.
- Choosing a well known tune and playing it in the key by ear.
- Encouraging pupils to talk about and describe the characteristics of a scale as if they were describing a friend (including particular fingerings and technical ingredients, key signature and any other interesting features).
- Playing scales in the style of the piece or in the style of the composer.

Left-brain activities

- Teaching the key signature.
- Teaching the note names.
- Teaching scales from notation.
- Writing scales down.
- Working at the technical elements.

I favour a way of teaching scales where 'playing the actual scale' comes very late on in the process. It's done by presenting pupils with a series of musically linked activities (based on the right- and left-brain activities above) over a period of perhaps three to four weeks (or longer) that gradually build up a holistic understanding and 'knowledge' of that scale[5]. The activities needn't come in any strict order – improvise and think *simultaneously*.

5 *Improve your scales!* (Faber Music) is based on these activities.

Teacher-led activities

- Play scales to your pupils making deliberate mistakes: pupils have to identify the errors.
- Teach simple and effective studies in the key.
- Compose short exercises, or teach suitable exercises or studies, that help pupils to overcome particular technical manoeuvres.

Pupil-based activities

Left brain

- What notes make up the scale? Learn to say them up and down.
- Learn to write down the key signature and the scale. (The benefits of teaching this thoroughly and methodically cannot be overstated.)
- Play the scale from notation, taking great care to prepare thoroughly first.

Right brain

- Hear the scale internally. Sing it out loud (perhaps begin with just the first three notes, then move to the first five, and finally to the whole scale), always pre-hearing each note first.
- Improvise and/or compose short phrases or tunes in the key.
- Choose a well-known tune and play it by ear in the key. Don't worry about mistakes – simply attempting to find the right notes is a very useful process.
- Talk about the scale: can pupils find three or four features that define that scale? (I call this activity 'scales as friends'.)

Practising scales in the imagination is also very helpful. No instrument is required, so it can be done anywhere, anytime. Research has shown that mental rehearsal of physical actions can be very effective. It's called 'motor imagery'. Imagine you're playing the scale: *think* the fingering and hear the notes internally. Athletes often practise this way and it can be a very powerful form of learning.

When pupils finally come to perform the scale proper, from memory and for the first time, make an event of it. Make sure that they are certain of the scale; there must be no doubt at this point. They either really know it or they don't. If they don't, go back and do more preparatory activities.

This method is a bit more involved than simply telling your pupils to go home and learn their scales but, if you are prepared to put in the time and effort, this kind of work will reap many rewards.

Play it as if ...

'As if' are two invaluable words. Use them often, for example:

- Play that note *as if* it's very close.
- Play that note *as if* it's very far away.
- Play that note *as if* you're turning the volume control up/down on your hi-fi.
- Play that note *as if* you had just seen a ghost.
- Play these notes *as if* they are hailstones bouncing on a roof.
- Play that phrase *as if* you're standing in the middle of a huge cathedral.
- Play that phrase *as if* you are going to sleep.
- Play that phrase *as if* you are in a bus driving over a bumpy road.
- Play that phrase *as if* you are in a punt drifting gently along a river.
- Play that phrase *as if* you are in a ferry crossing in a rough sea.
- Play that phrase *as if* you were the king or queen.

During a teaching day, occasionally try to take a moment out and listen to yourself at work. Ask yourself: 'am I using interesting enough language? Am I being really imaginative?'

The difference it will make to your pupils will be *as if* ...

Seeing the whole picture

In teaching pupils the Simultaneous way they will have identified, absorbed and mastered the ingredients, and understood the mood and character of a piece or song. Now they have to look beyond the details and begin to see the 'whole picture' in order to give a cohesive and musical performance. They have to make the transition from being 'inside looking out' to being 'outside looking in'. Just as we are able to see a cup and saucer, a painting, a tree or a building in a complete, holistic way, we need to do the same with music. Talk about the concept with pupils. Can they begin to see the piece as a whole? Mozart could 'see' *Don Giovanni* or *The Magic Flute* in an instant. We can begin to teach pupils to see their pieces in the same way. It requires imagination, a free and open mind, and a lot of right brain.

5 Practice makes perfect ... or does it?

More often than not, practice does just the opposite. Many pupils go home and play through their pieces (brain pretty much disengaged), each time cementing in more and more mistakes so that when the piece returns for the next lesson, it is considerably worse off than when it left at the end of the last one.

The word 'practice', like scales, is one of the most emotive in the musical language of the developing young musician. Some highly motivated children do seem to have the discipline to undertake regular and useful practice; others will need cajoling; and then there are those who (despite our finest efforts) don't quite seem to see the point of it at all.

If only all pupils could learn to make *some* decent use of all that time between lessons, what an effect it might have on their rate of progress.

Time for research

Why not indulge in a little research? Enlist a number of pupils (perhaps those you consider do have a certain amount of motivation and enthusiasm where practice is concerned) and ask them to make a really honest diary of a week's work. Ask them to note down the length of each practice session and exactly what they did – not what they would like you to think they did! Ask them to include what they particularly enjoyed practising and what they avoided. If they didn't practise ask them why not and don't allow such throwaway answers as 'I didn't have time'.

Pupils who produce a frank and candid practice diary could give you much food for thought and discussion. Perhaps this might inspire a group lesson with the same pupils, where an open exchange of views could take place. Now ask yourself how much time you devote to teaching pupils *how* to practise – and remember, there's a big difference between telling pupils *what* to practise and teaching them *how* to practise.

Most lessons last somewhere between twenty minutes and an hour. If lessons are weekly and held at a regular time, there are in fact 167 hours available for practice every week! Of course most of that time is taken up with day-to-day living but what an achievement it would be if pupils had a real desire to use *some* of those precious hours to practise because they really wanted to and to use that time in an effective, beneficial and creative way.

Re-evaluating practice

Let's re-evaluate practice and try to discover how it should fit into the teaching and learning process. There have been many chapters (and indeed whole books) written about practice and some of them contain many useful tips. Perhaps the problem that most of them don't really tackle is how to instil in our pupils a real *enthusiasm* for practice. How can we induce an approach that will encourage pupils to go home and want to get out their instruments and do at least *some* work?

It's very important that both pupil and teacher see practice as an integral part of progress – it should never be considered as an optional extra. A lesson should lead naturally on to practice and practice on to the next lesson; thus creating a continuous process that starts to create its own internal energy. How can we begin to achieve this marvellous ideal?

Let me pose four questions. The answers here are composite based on asking these questions many times in workshops. Before you read them, think first what answer you would give. At the end of this section we shall look at these questions again.

Q1) Why do pupils need to practise?

Q2) What do we expect pupils to do?

Q3) How do we communicate our wishes?

Q4) How do we motivate our pupils to practise?

A1) To get better.

A2) (Average answer) a piece or two and a couple of scales.

A3) Ticks in the tutor book or make a list in the notebook.

A4) 'Well, if you don't you'll fail your exam!'

Practice as a re-creation of the lesson

There is much to be said for recreating the lesson during practice: it gives practice a structure. If we are conscientious, we tell pupils to begin with some warms-ups, play some scales and then work carefully on the pieces, correcting mistakes as they go along or perhaps doing the hard bits first. This is not always as successful as we might think. The energy, effort and self-discipline required (for most pupils) to approach practice in this manner is often more than they might have. It all seems simply too daunting and so the end result is either no practice at all, or something that represents no more than a token gesture.

Making that quantum leap

The difficulty that most pupils need to overcome is that initial feeling of having to stop whatever they are doing – playing computer/video games, sending text messages, watching the television, chatting on their mobiles, doing the *Times* crossword, eating, doing all these things at the same time (or even doing their homework!) – and then find the physical and psychological energy to get their instrument out of its case (or open the piano lid) and begin. We have to find a way to remove that initial psychological barrier of how to get started.

I believe the answer is simple. Just as our lessons begin without opening the book (so removing the anxiety that often accompanies seeing all that complex notation), practice will also begin in the same way. It is so much less threatening. Encourage pupils to think about the activities they did at the lesson (there's a novel thought – practice begins with *thinking*!) and then decide what they would like to achieve in the forthcoming practice session.

> A little more work on the key we were exploring, which was G major; some more improvisations in G major, using that rhythmic pattern – 'I like pineapple ice cream'; using f and p; all in a 'bluesy' sort of a mood.

And so practice begins – mistakes can't be made and the right brain is turned on. Ideas from the lesson are being developed through interesting and creative musical activity without the notation but based on the piece introduced earlier.

As this kind of practice develops, it becomes important that pupils are clearly aware of the ingredients that make up their pieces. They must really try to remember those you introduced in the first lesson on a new piece (see *A couple of golden rules*, page 15) but after that they should learn to write down the ingredients themselves.

Be a detective

[6] Published by Faber Music.

Improve your practice![6] has space for pupils to write down the ingredients of eight pieces. Each of the five graded books has slightly more sophisticated questions for pupils to answer, allowing them to build up a picture of their pieces. It doesn't take long – perhaps a couple of boxes are filled out each session. How many times have I adjudicated at festivals and asked performers 'now, without looking at the music, can you tell me what your piece was called?' Blank look. That, of course, explains why there was little sense of style and character in their performance. Using *Improve your practice!* pupils can be encouraged to be detectives and really get to know their pieces properly. It's a bit of simple analysis really (but don't say so!). Opposite is an example of how pupils will explore a piece from a grade one book.

Each of the *Improve your practice!* books also has twenty-four activity cards – twelve *without music* activities and twelve *with music*. Pupils deal themselves one or two and carry out whatever the card says. It's like playing a game. The activities are based on making connections between the piece and all the various areas of music discussed in our original Simultaneous Learning model. Some connect with the right brain and some with the left. Straight away, practice is a much more positive activity. Just as the Simultaneous Learning *sliding scale* (see page 21) generates an infinite number of ways to deliver a lesson, this idea encourages pupils to vary the way they work during practice. Sometimes they can spend the whole time on an imaginative voyage of musical discovery and sometimes they can do some very specific and detailed work. Often pupils can make practice a combination of the two (perhaps even occasionally beginning at bar one!).

Explore your piece

See page 24 for help

1. Title
2. Composer
3. Period
4. What does the title tell you about the music?
5. What key is the piece in?
6. Write the key signature here (including the clef)
7. Are there any scale and arpeggio patterns in the music?
8. In which bars do they occur?
9. What is the time signature?
10. What will you count?

All these answers form the 'ingredients' of your piece. If you don't understand a question, don't worry; just remember to ask your teacher in your next lesson.

11. Write down all the dynamics that occur, including *dim.* and *cresc.* List them in order of soft – loud:
12. Write down any other markings (such as staccato, slurs, accents etc.) and their meanings:
13. Write down some words that describe the mood of the piece:
14. Find out something interesting about the composer:
15. Are there any tricky rhythms in this piece? Write them down here, and then clap them:
16. Is there anything particularly challenging in the piece? Which bars will need special practice?

4

5

After warm-ups, pupils should play some musical games with the appropriate ingredients (with the music book still closed). The cards encourage the following kind of activities, perhaps two to be played with each piece:

Activities without the music

- Choose two or three of the piece's ingredients and using them make up a short and simple piece.
- Practise the scale and arpeggio of the piece slowly, with your best tone quality and in the style of the piece.
- Think about the title of the piece. Make up a short and simple piece using the same title.
- Practise any bar (or bars) that you can from memory with your eyes closed.
- Using the time signature of the piece make up a simple rhythm and write it down.

In this way, practice immediately begins as a creative activity and pupils have to think about the ingredients that make up their piece (rather than just playing it through in a half-hearted and thought-*less* manner, complete with ever growing numbers of uncorrected mistakes). They are undertaking real 'musical activity' and learning the piece without actually playing it. They are thinking in the key and making up their own exercises to overcome technical problems. As a result, practice becomes a much more pupil-directed activity with the pupil taking ownership of their own progress. Suddenly, it also becomes more stimulating and easier to begin, because there is nothing to get wrong.

After a while, the music book can be opened and other activities chosen from a second group:

Activities with the music

- Choose a passage and play it loudly; quietly; with a *crescendo*; with a *diminuendo*; as written and then from memory.
- Hear the piece through in your head as best you can.
- Choose a tricky bar and make up an exercise to help you practise it.
- Play the piece (or part of the piece) through, ignoring all the dynamic markings.
- Choose a bar or two and play the chosen bar or bars starting one octave higher or lower.
- Make up a story to fit the music.
- Choose a passage or section of the piece and practise playing it with as much character and expression as possible.

The special ingredient

Encourage pupils, as the week's practice unfolds, to identify one special feature that will be given particular prominence in the week's practice. It might be a scale (or the first five notes of a scale); a technical challenge that has been overcome; an improvisation that has grown into a composition; part of a piece that is going really well; a complete piece; or just the first note of a piece which can now be played with great character and quality – it doesn't matter what. The results can be spectacular.

First, pupils' minds are focused on what they are achieving and because that feature becomes their special ingredient the extra attention it receives will result in even more progress. Once we've discovered the special ingredient and given it due praise, we might then allow the next part of the lesson to unfold based upon it. This can do wonders for pupils' self-esteem. The fact that you, their respected and admired teacher, deem their work worthy enough to use in generating the next part of the lesson may have a significant effect. One teacher, who was using this strategy, came back to me with this lovely story. A very average pupil came to a lesson with a short improvisation as her special ingredient – nothing remarkable but certainly commendable. 'Very well done,' said the teacher and then did something that dramatically changed that pupil's musical life. The teacher went to the next studio (this happened in a school) and asked her friend, teaching next door, to pop in for thirty seconds and listen to this piece. 'Very nice indeed,' said the second teacher. This average pupil was so enthused by having two authority figures praising her that she never looked back. She didn't turn into a Brendel or an Ashkenazy but her piano playing improved out of all recognition. I'm not suggesting that this will always happen – but you just never know!

Using the special ingredient to generate part of the lesson in the Simultaneous Learning manner makes a very strong link between practice and lesson. If you use the idea on a regular basis it can also set up an energy, which, if successfully engaged, will positively snowball. The whole practice-lesson-practice-lesson routine really begins to work and you will have a highly motivated pupil.

'Now that Kathryn's grade two, I expect she should be practising for fourteen-and-a-half minutes ... '

Parents always want to know for how long their child should be practising. Don't tell them! Instead tell them that Kathryn should decide what she wants to achieve and then practise for as long as that takes. It may be five minutes or thirty-five but if Kathryn sets out with clear objectives she won't be spending the time clock-watching and time filling. A rather shrewd young trumpet player was told by his parents that he had to practise for twenty minutes a day. A piece he quite liked lasted five minutes, so he played it four times each day and that was his twenty minutes. Everyone was happy except his teacher. He never seemed to make any progress for all the practice he did.

Teach your pupils to monitor their practice. It's very helpful in giving it direction and purpose. After about five minutes pupils should think: 'is it going well? Am I achieving what I set out to?' They should ask themselves again after another five minutes. Perhaps you might teach them to 'TEP' – think, evaluate, plan – as a regular part of their practice. It only takes a few seconds but can really help to keep a practice session in focus.

'I did set out to practise but I was so tired on Monday and Wednesday and Thursday and ... '

Here are some ideas for those tired pupils:

- Sit in a comfortable chair with some music and hear it in your head. (The rhythm at least, if not the melody.)
- Imagine yourself playing a scale – think through the fingering carefully and then play it slowly in your head, imagining the fingering really strongly.
- Listen to some music – a recording of the piece you're learning, a pop song, the theme tune to a TV programme, anything. Then write a sentence or two about it, referring to instruments, dynamics, smooth or detached playing and so on.
- Do a 'PEP' analysis. Choose a piece and find that comfortable chair again, then think through the following:
  - **P** is for problems: decide what problems you still have to solve – technical or rhythmic perhaps. Make a note of them.
  - **E** is for expression: what will you be trying to convey in your performance?
  - **P** is for practice: the *next* practice! What in particular will you work on in your next session? Write your intentions down.

Practice in the head can be very effective. Pupils are often sufficiently energised by thinking about practice in these ways that they actually get up and do some!

Let's now revisit those questions from the beginning of the chapter again and see if we can come up with a better set of answers:

Q1) Why do pupils need to practise?

A1) To process and make sense of the lesson; to make connections with their present understanding which will lead to a greater understanding; to begin engaging that lesson-practice energy.

Q2) What do we expect pupils to do?

A2) THINK! Use their imaginations and begin to develop the work of the lesson.

Q3) How do we communicate our wishes?

A3) Through very careful preparation in the lesson and continual reference to how pupils can further develop the content of the lesson on their own.

Q4) How do we motivate our pupils to practise?

A4) By being imaginative and enthusiastic, and presenting practice as a very desirable, exciting, entertaining and absorbing activity.

By spending some quality time teaching our pupils about it, practice becomes an integral part of the ongoing learning process. Practice and the lesson connect, we remove that often overwhelming sense of difficulty in getting started, we cause the imagination to play a major role and we end up encouraging our pupils to use this precious time in a truly musical way.

6 The first lessons

The first lessons can be so crucial to a musician's potential development. It is good fortune being able to teach a pupil from the very first lesson – sometimes when inheriting pupils we may have to spend a fair number of lessons putting things right before we can begin to go forward with any impetus. (Though we should never let on to pupils – they may have adored their previous teacher, even though damage may have been done.)

What should we do in those first couple of lessons? Their importance cannot be overstated. Pupils are at their most enthusiastic, so it's a time to sow some quality seeds. Obviously, in specific terms, what we do will depend on what instrument we are teaching but I'd like to suggest one or two general principles that always ought to be part of those first lessons.

Posture

In whatever manner you present it or whatever language you use, good posture is vital. Pupils who, from the start, play or sing with a tension free posture are highly advantaged. I have seen so many young players struggle because of poor posture.

Improvisation

There are ways of getting some kind of interesting sounds from most instruments in the first lesson – use them to do some free improvisation. Imagine Ben, a new and extremely enthusiastic piano pupil. He comes bouncing into his first lesson with that treasure house of sounds (the piano) sitting there tantalisingly in front of him, crying out to be explored, and his first musical experience is:

'What about the other 999 notes?' he's probably thinking. I'm sure he'd rather be playing (improvising) 'Dinosaurs' or 'Space travel'.

However, watch out for Aunt Mildred who may have been brought up in a rather different world. A friend told me this rather sad story: young Francesca had been learning the piano for a few weeks with a bright, enthusiastic and imaginative teacher. As well as learning pieces from 'My first piano tutor', she was very excited by making up her own music. Along came Sunday afternoon and a visit from Aunt Mildred. Young Fran couldn't wait to give a performance of her very own 'Elephants go for a walk' with big splashy *ff* chords in the bass and lots of dissonant, thumpy note clusters. Fran ended with a flourish and an expectant grin. 'Hmm,' responded Aunt Mildred, 'I thought you were going to play me a proper piece.' The moral is: make sure you tell Aunt Mildred about the ways of the modern world, between the roast beef and the apple pie.

Notation

Whatever teaching materials you're going to use, make sure that you employ Simultaneous Learning processes from the very start. Let's say that the tutor book you're using does happen to have 'I'll have cake' as its first piece. Make strong connections with basic pulse and rhythm. Play some call-and-response clapping games using the rhythm, and play call-and-response games on the piano. Play some question-and-answer games using the rhythm and simple one or two note patterns, all over the piano. You could even make up your own words to fit the phrase.

Now, finally, put the tutor book on the stand. Look at the phrase and sing it (perhaps you first and then pupils). Now look at it again and ask your pupils to hear it in their head. (For those who may need some extra stages to understand this concept, first get them to hear a spoken sentence in their head. Then they might hear a long, sustained sound – like a siren – before the actual musical phrase you wish them to hear.) Finally, they play it from the notation. Then your pupils repeat the phrase, firstly singing along as they play (on a stringed instrument or the piano), then again hearing it in their head as they play.

In this way you are developing that hugely important skill – looking at music and being able to know what it sounds like in the head – *from the very first lesson.*

Thereafter, whenever you work at anything from notation make sure that you follow this sequence:

Notational symbol ⟶ SOUND (singing/hearing internally) ⟶ Play

You'll be developing a considerably more *musical* pupil.

Send your pupil home to make up another, similar piece using the same rhythm but perhaps using two or three notes. Maybe encourage them to write it down and then use this to generate the first part of the second lesson.

Try to encourage pupils to write something down in every lesson and practice session, be it a single note, a melodic pattern, a rhythmic pattern, a musical symbol. It's that crucial third element of musical language – read, play and *write* – and is tremendously important in aiding holistic understanding.

Whatever you do, be especially imaginative in those first few lessons.

7 Sight-reading

I'm including some thoughts on sight-reading in this book (which otherwise deals with teaching and learning processes and principles rather than specific teaching topics) because of its major importance in musical development. When a pupil can sight-read music fluently, not only do they do well in exams but (rather more importantly) it also frees up much of our teaching time, allowing us to concentrate on developing *the musician*. (In using the expression 'sight-reading', I don't just mean playing a sight-reading test – as in an exam – but any interaction with notation.)

When children learn their language, the three elements of speaking, reading and writing are strongly linked, allowing them to communicate, think, learn and develop in their own chosen fashion. Let's see to it that the same is true when we teach the language of music. We must do our best to make sure that reading, alongside playing, is not going to hold back our pupils. Let's also make sure that the third element, writing, has its place too.

Look at this short piece for 30 seconds:

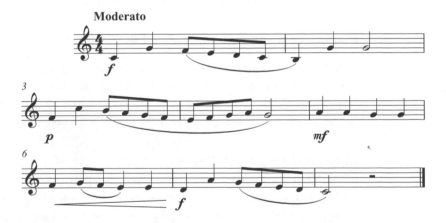

Now look away. If you're by an instrument, try playing the tune (no looking at the notes!). If not, try re-playing it through in your head. I imagine you were pretty accurate. You looked at the music, *understood what you saw*, got the (musical) point and so it probably popped straight into your memory, allowing you to give a fairly accurate rendition almost immediately. Our pupils can be taught to do that too. It takes time but it certainly can be done and it's very worthwhile.

Let's spend a moment thinking about how we sight-read, before considering how best to teach the skill.

Snap!

First of all there's the eye. It's a very powerful piece of equipment and can take in a lot of information in a very short space of time – scientists tell us that we can read up to four words in one-hundredth of a second! The eye works pretty much like a camera; you look at something and take a snapshot. Most of you will be taking about four or five snapshots as you read each line of this page, taking in between three and five words at a 'snap' (or saccade, if you'd like the technical term).

The next stage – *understanding* what we read – is a procedure that combines the eye and the brain. Images are perceived by the eye and then processed by the brain. If we have the appropriate 'software', then we understand. As we read these words, we can also say them, both internally and out loud. We know what they mean (without having to say them out loud) and we could write them down later. It's the same with music but we have to have the appropriate software installed. For example, read the following sentence:

Легко читать в виде

Maybe it didn't make too much sense, if we're not up with our Russian. Translated it says 'Sight-reading is easy' but if we can't understand the symbols and the language, it's meaningless. Successful sight-reading works when we understand what it is that we're reading, so we have to teach pupils to understand what they see. We do that by being really thorough, ensuring that pupils really absorb and digest what we teach them, making relevant connections as they go along – especially with aural, rhythm, scales and theory.

Preparing a pupil to sight-read some music

This may be for a practice 'sight-reading' test, or it may be just for reading music during the normal course of playing. Let's begin to approach the two in the same way. There are three basic areas to attend to and each must be secure before giving the green light to go ahead and play the piece.

Notes and melodic patterns

Pupils MUST know the notes and where to find them or how to play them (depending on the instrument). There must be no thinking time – from symbol to physical action in a flash. Pupils must also be aware of patterns. Music is full of patterns – point them out, teach your pupils to recognise them. They will always be there, particularly the sort of melodic patterns that are as common as words such as 'the' or 'and'. These kinds of shapes should elicit an immediate response. Pupils should *know* them as if they were a completely familiar word or phrase. Patterns, for example, like:

Rhythm

Thorough work on rhythm will pay great dividends. There's no reason why any pupil should have a problem with rhythm, if taught thoroughly. There are only two aspects to rhythm – pulse and sub-division. Teach both carefully (in whatever ways you favour), ensuring that pupils really know how a rhythm sounds before they play it.

Technique

Finally, make sure that there is nothing that might cause a technical problem. Perhaps there's an awkward fingering, a change of hand position, a tricky interval to pitch. Work it out carefully first. Practise it.

A golden rule and the big moment

You're about to give the green light, your pupil is about to play. The golden rule is this:

> **Don't let pupils begin unless you are almost entirely sure that they will get it right.**

Careful, thorough preparation is crucial. Let's see what happens? The pupil plays, gets it right and thinks, 'That wasn't so bad, let's try another one!' This is *positive motivation* in action, following a simple motivational model:

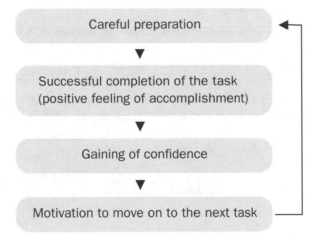

This is a very different result compared to what might happen when presenting a sight-reading test with no preparation – the pupil struggles through; there is no sense of pulse or rhythm; wrong notes by the fistful, all of which result in no positive feelings of achievement, just the fostering of an increasing dislike and fear of sight-reading.

'With all that preparation, was it really sight-reading?' you ask. Yes, it was and that preparation is essential to build up confidence, fluency and accuracy. The final performance was still the first time the piece was read complete, so psychologically it is being sight-read. Very gradually you will reduce the preparation time, so by the time pupils are about to take an exam, for example, they will have the necessary confidence to play with understanding, accuracy and fluency.

Multi-tasking

Sight-reading is very much a multi-tasking activity, rather like driving or playing tennis or computer games. It requires strong simultaneous connections with a number of other areas. Concentrate on one or two of the following each time you work with pupils on reading. (Obviously, when working with dyslexic pupils, allowances will have to be made as there is only a certain amount of information that they can process at any one time.)

Aural

Ultimately we want pupils, like we do, to look at music and understand what they see. We would like them to think 'I know what that's about.' This takes us back to the beginning, for if we teach notation (as suggested on page 50) at the very first lesson, then we are always going to have a much more musically perceptive pupil. Get pupils used to hearing music in their heads – encourage them, for example, to take their music on a car journey or on holiday, to read alongside their reading books. If they can't hear the melody at first, they can at least begin with the rhythm. Just like reading words, pupils don't have to play music out loud to 'hear' what it sounds like.

Verbalising

Grasping the 'meaning' of a musical pattern will only work when the pattern is musically understood. We can find out how pupils are processing what they see by asking appropriate questions or suggesting that they give a running commentary on the music. In this way the snapshot technique really begins to work. They will begin to connect appropriate notes into patterns and then read these patterns at a glance, which will aid fluency enormously.

Look at this next phrase:

Perceiving the patterns is so important. So, when describing this phrase, I'd like a pupil to say something along the lines of 'it begins with a two-note descending pattern (they can add that the notes are E and D and crotchets but that's not so important), then there's an ascending C major arpeggio pattern followed by a repeat of the first pattern an octave higher and then the previous arpeggio pattern, this time descending'.

The eye would need one glance per pattern. The brain processes the patterns and sends the appropriate messages to the fingers and the passage is played fluently and in time (if it's being read by a pianist then a further connection with arpeggio fingering is made). Always guide pupils into noticing these patterns. The more they look, the more they find. Once they are reading patterns, we can neatly move on to ...

Reading ahead

Perceiving these patterns and reading them at a glance will (with virtually no extra help) cause readers to look ahead naturally. We occasionally hear about virtuoso readers who can read many bars or even half a page (or more) ahead! When we look at music, our eyes can move up to about five or six times per second – scanning the music, building up a picture of what's there to be seen and processed. If we tell our pupils to 'look ahead', we are, in effect, helping them to kick-start this important scanning process. Otherwise they may simply read lazily. You don't need to prescribe how far to look ahead, just talk about the procedure. Pupils will find their own natural pace.

Remembering the key

The process of sight-reading uses up quite a bit of short-term memory. We take in a snapshot of musical information, process it, memorise it and play it, while our eyes are taking the next snapshot and repeating the process. All that happens in virtually a split second, so we don't want to overload the memory with extra information, especially trying to remember the key signature as we go along. We want to teach our pupils to 'think in the key' and there are two ways to help them.

Firstly, as you use more Simultaneous Learning techniques, 'thinking in keys' will begin to happen more naturally. Secondly, make sure that one of the major connections, when teaching scales, is with notation. As well as learning our scales from memory we need to know *what they look like*. Writing out the scale may be beneficial, thus maintaining an important link with theory, and we must learn scales *with* the music as well as from memory. Not only will we become more adept at recognising scale patterns (which helps fluency) but we are also beginning to 'programme' keys securely into the brain.

Fingering

Similarly, learning scales and arpeggios from notation is a great help with fingering. Pianists often run out of fingers; string players find themselves in the wrong position; wind players get into a tangle with alternative keys. If scales and related patterns are learnt from notation, pupils will instinctively know what to do. All being well, the appropriate fingering will then just flow naturally into their minds.

Observing markings

If pupils have been brought up to think simultaneously, then observing the various markings should be no problem. They will be assimilated, musically understood and should be incorporated into the performance. However, sometimes some old-fashioned nagging may be the answer! Do insist that markings are followed. The eye has no problem in taking them in.

Sight-reading methods

There are a number of ways to teach pupils to sight-read and we need to do so actively. Some pupils seem to be naturally good sight-readers but most will need a lot of help. You might have a pile of music set aside for sight-reading – if you do, make sure that it is very well graded. Just giving pupils something to read will not help them unless it is carefully chosen. One session struggling through a piece that is too hard can set a pupil back a long way. There are a number of 'methods' available, one being *Improve your sight-reading!*[7] in which I have presented a sequential, cumulative series of stages to build up sight-reading ability from lesson one through to grade eight and beyond. If you do choose to follow this method, the next sections detail how best to use it.

[7] Published by Faber Music.

Rhythm exercises

Each stage begins with some rhythm exercises. These *must* be fully grasped before moving on – it is vital that pupils know how rhythms work. Work at sustaining a steady pulse initially. Always hear the rhythms in the head first, tapping the pulse and hearing the rhythm internally. There are many ways of doing these exercises and pupils should have experience of them all. For example:

[8] It's particularly important to hear rhythms internally (sustaining the note lengths) when clapping, to clarify the idea that notes have length. Otherwise all notes sound the same (i.e. the length of the clap).

- Tap the pulse with your right foot (sometimes use your left foot) and clap the rhythm (consciously hearing it in your head at the same time)[8].
- Tap the pulse with one hand and the rhythm with the other (then swap hands).
- Tap the pulse with your foot and play the rhythm on one note.
- Tap the pulse with your foot and make up a tune to fit the rhythm.

Always count in: preferably four bars – two out loud and then two internally (which means that you can monitor whether the counting is in time). Make sure the rhythm exercises are *really* understood before moving on to the next section.

Melodic exercises

When preparing melodic exercises first check for technical problems and iron them out. Next, make sure the rhythm is absolutely understood. Pupils should then work through the following:

- Clap the exercise, at the same time hearing the rhythm in the head.
- Think about the key. Play the scale and arpeggio from memory and from notation (have a scale book handy whenever you're working with pupils on sight-reading).
- Hear the piece in the head again, this time with the melody as well. (Give the first note to help. It may not be too accurate at first but pupils will soon improve. For those pupils who are a little uncertain about 'hearing music in their heads' just ask them to sing 'Happy birthday' (or any familiar tune) silently – in their heads – they'll soon get the idea!)

Working methodically through all the melodic exercises in all the books is rather like building up a musical vocabulary. Pupils will meet and come to recognise melodic patterns that recur again and again, just as they do with words and phrases when reading text.

Prepared pieces

Work through the questions to encourage pupils to 'see and understand' the piece. Make sure that all patterns are noticed. Sometimes ask pupils to give you a 'running commentary' on the music. Ask pupils whether they feel they know what they are about to play. Don't allow a pupil to begin unless you are (almost completely) certain the performance will be correct. Once played, ask your pupil to evaluate the performance. With careful preparation there should have been no errors or hesitation. If there were, however, follow with a short discussion and a second performance.

Unprepared pieces

'Unprepared pieces' does not mean they should be played without preparation. It is now up to pupils to discover the clues to each piece. Give them roughly a minute to look at (read through) and 'understand' the music. Pupils must learn to check rhythms and other technical features, and always try to hear the music in their heads. Gradually reduce the preparation time. Eventually, with very careful methodical practice, your pupil should be able to scan the music for thirty seconds or so and know what it's all about, allowing for confident and accurate playing – just as you were able to do with that piece we first looked at on page 51.

Sight-reading musically

Whenever we speak, we put expression into what we say (without exception), whatever our mood. It's a point you might like to discuss with your pupils. Similarly, whenever we play music, it should be both expressive and characterful. That includes playing sight-reading pieces. As a start it's important to follow the markings – but this is only a start; there are other considerations.

As pupils read the piece through in their head, encourage them to evolve an idea of its character and of how they will interpret the music. For example, does it require a crisp, rhythmic approach or more gentle, sustained playing? Will the first beats need accenting, or playing without emphasis? Does it require a fairly strict pulse, or would a degree of freedom be appropriate? Pianists need to consider whether the texture is tune and accompaniment, or whether both hands are of equal importance. Encourage pupils to look for the clues and then play accordingly. They should never play blandly.

Teaching sight-reading without (much) sight-reading!

If you have a group of pupils moving towards a grade exam, get them together for a group lesson on sight-reading, perhaps once or twice a term. This sight-reading group session has a rather neat twist – very little actual sight-reading will be taking place (pupils generally like the idea of this). You'll just be working at the various skills that have to come together to make a good sight-reader. I call these 'sight-reading warm-ups'. Such a session can generate a great deal of fun.

The lesson, up to an hour long (and finishing with drinks and chocolate biscuits – or fruit), should go something like this:

9 See: *Dalcroze Today*, by Marie-Laure Bachmann (OUP), for more information. It's a fascinating read.

- **Rise and shine:** drink a glass of water. Think about and work on a well-balanced, tension-free posture; work on relaxation. Perhaps include some brain exercises. Pupils learn to create a positive mental and physical mind-set in relation to sight-reading.
- **Playing ball:** rhythm exercises and games – pulse and sub-division games, hearing rhythms in the head, clapping and, yes, even playing ball! (Have a look at some Dalcroze activities[9].)
- **Sing along:** melodic exercises – singing intervals (melodically and harmonically) and short phrases. Try getting your hands on and singing exercises from *333 Elementary exercises in sight singing* by Kodály.
- **Multi-tasking:** clapping and singing at the same time.
- **In your head:** for example, pupils might study *and memorise* a short phrase (internally). Then you play it with a deliberate wrong note – pupils have to identify the note. Prepare some well-known tunes and write them on manuscript paper – a prize for whoever recognises them first.
- **'Ear' ear:** make a connection with old-fashioned aural, where you play and pupils *write it down*. Always use very simple and short melodic phrases – the kind of musical patterns that constitute regularly occurring 'musical vocabulary'. It's a powerful connection and, if presented in the right way, can be fun.
- **Time for talking:** pupils talk through pieces, spotting patterns, finding the clues to a musical performance, all the time developing the ability to understand and articulate what they see.
- **Putting it all together:** looking at a sight-reading exercise as a whole for a minute or so and feeling confident that it is understood, learning the rules of thorough preparation. Perhaps even do some sight-reading at this stage!

Do set aside some quality time to *teach* your pupils to sight-read – they'll be very grateful in the long run. It's very much a part of giving your pupils musical independence.

8 Group teaching

Many of the problems associated with group teaching dissolve almost completely if you use Simultaneous Learning. It will enable you to keep two, three, four (or even more) children happily occupied and musically challenged – even if the mission to deliver an effective, musical, pacey and absorbing lesson is compounded by a group that is distinctly not that well-matched in standard, temperament or instrument.

However, we must hope that in most cases our groups *are* reasonably well matched. Supervisors should certainly try their very best to avoid really disparate groups – in such circumstances the quality of the teaching would inevitably be a little compromised over an extended period. Do raise the matter with the appropriate powers-that-be if you feel that a group is simply too diverse. It benefits no one otherwise.

Giving a group lesson

Assuming we have, for example, three or four flute players, violinists or clarinettists of similar standard, or perhaps three trumpets and a trombone, how do we apply the process of Simultaneous Learning? I've seen occasional group lessons that are really nothing more than three or four individual lessons packed into a twenty- or thirty-minute slot. Each pupil gets about five minutes of (less than top quality) time and the rest fiddle about. So, not like that!

Good quality group teaching will inevitably require a little careful planning. You will need to know your ingredients well, for example. Imagine we have a group of four beginner clarinettists. Tom is a little quicker than the rest (and practises very enthusiastically) and Tim is a little slower on the up-take. They all have the same well-chosen tutor book (and a copy of *Improve your practice!*) and have been learning for a term.

Today's lesson is going to begin by revisiting the piece (in G major) that you began last week. The ingredients are clearly in your mind.

As pupils enter, you are already generating a gentle $\frac{4}{4}$ pulse. It's up to you how you do this because you've also got to chat to them about the hamsters! Perhaps a quiet foot tapping or a hidden metronome is a possibility (see page 16). When instruments are ready, have pupils form a circle with you as part of it. (As much group teaching takes place in schools, good relations are important – you need an appropriately sized room and you may have to move things around a bit.)

Begin with some warm-ups (the pulse is still discernible – do your warm-ups in time). Then move on to some call-and-response work. 'I want your tone today to be full and rich like chocolate fudge cake.' You play G for four beats. They respond as a group. Repeat twice, f first and then p.

Choose other notes, gradually building up a G major scale. Bring in two- and three-note legato scale patterns (from the piece). Now direct your call-and-response to individual pupils, indicating exactly who is to respond *during* the call. Keep the pulse going throughout. Allow pupils a second go if they didn't get a response correct – without commenting, if possible. However, do comment if you want to make a point more strongly or use a member of the group as an example ('that note was a bit bumpy!'; 'Your shoulders are a bit stiff!'; 'Look at how well Tim is holding his shoulders', etc.). Ask questions ('what does legato mean?'; 'What key are we playing in?' etc.), always waiting for the answers.

'Now,' you ask Tom, 'what is your special ingredient this week?'

'A two-bar phrase which I've composed based on three ingredients from the piece' comes the delighted reply. 'Can you play it to us?' He does and that leads you into some question-and-answer work based on Tom's phrase (which of course is itself based on the ingredients of the piece). Now Tom is going to lead some more question-and-answer work. Tom does (he's done so before), very successfully.

Now let's concentrate on the dynamics for a bit and add a new dynamic level (from the piece). 'Tim, can you lead us through some long note work including the new dynamic, using the first five notes of G major?' Tim does (he's done it before), very successfully. 'Now let's write down that new dynamic level in our notebooks …' and so the session continues.

It's a Simultaneous Learning lesson where all are engaged continuously and musically and each at their own level. Perhaps that's only taken about six or seven minutes of the lesson but we've covered an awful lot. Both Tom and Tim have been allowed to take centre stage; there will be time for the other two to do so as well later on. No one is daunted by the work as we've been doing this kind of thing since lesson one.

There will be times when you will devote a longer period to a particular pupil. The others can be watching and perhaps commenting, or practising the same phrase silently, practising in their heads or writing something down in their manuscript books or notebooks, or Tom may be helping Tim while you work with the other two for a couple of minutes. Sometimes a lesson will be predominantly on the totally organic Simultaneous Learning end of the sliding scale, sometimes it will be at the highly detailed study end, or it may be anywhere in between.

The important point is that these pupils are being continuously musically occupied and are supporting each other throughout the duration of the lesson. You are firmly in control, directing the lesson confidently – not in a hurry, allowing each pupil to play his or her part and build up confidence.

At some point, the book will make an appearance (preferably with one music stand between two). Make connections with all the work you've been doing so far – don't begin at bar one just because it happens to be at the beginning of the piece! Only begin there if you mean to for a reason.

Continually make reference to practice.

Sometimes you will wish to work at ensemble music. Perhaps the group is to play in a concert or is preparing for a Music Medals exam. Again, preliminary work takes place using the ingredients and this might continue for two, three or more weeks before you introduce the notation. Once introduced, don't assign a line to a pupil at first; all pupils should learn and play all parts. There are other 'behavioural' concepts of ensemble playing to teach too: watching, listening, leading, thinking and playing together *as one*. Use your imagination and you'll come up with all sorts of fun activities to establish these ideas. Here's one I like:

Line your pupils up, each standing next to the other, on one side of the room. They have to get to the other side at exactly the same time, using exactly the same steps and maintaining the line exactly. No one is allowed to talk. Don't tell them how to do it, just say 'go!'

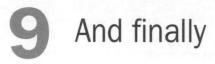

9 And finally ...

Building confidence, taking risks

Success as a teacher, a learner, a musician comes in no small measure from confidence. I don't mean that kind of overt confidence born of arrogance. I mean a kind of quiet, empowering, inner confidence and self-belief that develops slowly but surely and results in poise, humility and self-assurance.

How can we achieve this? As part of our own self-development it will result from taking pride in our work – from dipping into appropriate professional development, be it simply reading a book and trying out new ideas, attending courses, or embarking on one of the more extensive professional development qualifications.

As far as our pupils are concerned, it's very much to do with how we treat them. Much praise where it's due is vital (good teaching sets up praise-worthy opportunities on a regular basis) and creating an environment where pupils can say 'I don't understand' or 'I still can't do it', with no fear of being made to feel stupid or inferior, is essential. In fact, pupils are made to feel better learners for being honest. They are simply calling on our trust and expertise to find more effective solutions for them. As creative, imaginative teachers, and by making the appropriate connections, we will be able to provide those solutions.

It is this that begins to create confidence in our pupils: confidence in their learning and confidence in their performing. They will begin to take risks; 'I wonder what will happen if I try it like this?' They might fall flat on their faces (metaphorically) but they'll soon get up and have another go. They'll want to try more challenging pieces, play faster, slower, quieter, louder ... you may find both you and your pupils seem to be on a helter-skelter ride and that teaching and learning suddenly become addictive.

Personalising your curriculum

Draw on your imagination and creative powers to formulate your curriculum. If you are teaching the Simultaneous way, you'll find that you can get through a lot of repertoire – choose from a wide variety of music, challenge pupils when you think appropriate, always make connections. Don't be in a hurry – always teach thoroughly and there's no need to rely on exams to set your teaching agenda. Use them by all means but as a means to an end, not as ends in themselves. Occasionally take time out for an exam but look upon these as milestones not goals. Our aim must be to produce rounded, enthusiatic and independent musicians in whose lives music will always play an important part.

What's the point again?

If we are prepared to change and to assimilate some Simultaneous Learning ideas into our teaching, we might find many fascinating and exciting transformations taking place – both in the way we teach and in the way our pupils learn. That in itself may inspire us to search out even more interesting and different routes.

Let's briefly summarise the potential benefits from such teaching:

- It brings the imagination to the foreground of teaching.
- It encourages lessons to flow more spontaneously.
- It encourages pupils to take a much more active part in their own learning.
- It leads to 'musical thinking'.
- It encourages whole brain, holistic thinking.
- It offers an exciting alternative to compartmentalised teaching.
- It introduces many more areas of musical learning into the lesson.
- It puts aural at the centre of musical learning.
- It teaches musical 'ingredients' so that pupils learn effectively, allowing them to apply their understanding more successfully.
- It improves the quality of practice.
- It encourages greater positive motivation – both pupil and teacher are less likely to become bored.
- Ultimately it produces independent musical thinkers, so the likelihood of giving up is reduced and more people out there can be given the opportunity to live enriched lives through the power of making music.

Yes, it takes a little more time! And yes, you'll have to think a bit more about what you're doing. But don't deny your pupils that time; it's time well spent. All children have music within them. Some will go far, further perhaps than certain kinds of old-fashioned methods would have allowed. Some, who otherwise might have given up very early on, may find their own way into our astonishing world through styles of teaching we may have formerly resisted, or didn't even know we could draw upon.

Dare to be different and once committed to change, remain open-minded, always on the search for fresh ideas and new ways forward.

We can all be great teachers if we want to be. I hope you will.